Headlines in History

San Pedro Bay

Area

Photo Research by
Charles F. Queenan

"Chronicles of Enterprise" by
Cynthia Simone

Produced in Cooperation with the
Los Angeles Maritime Museum

Windsor Publications, Inc.
Chatsworth, California

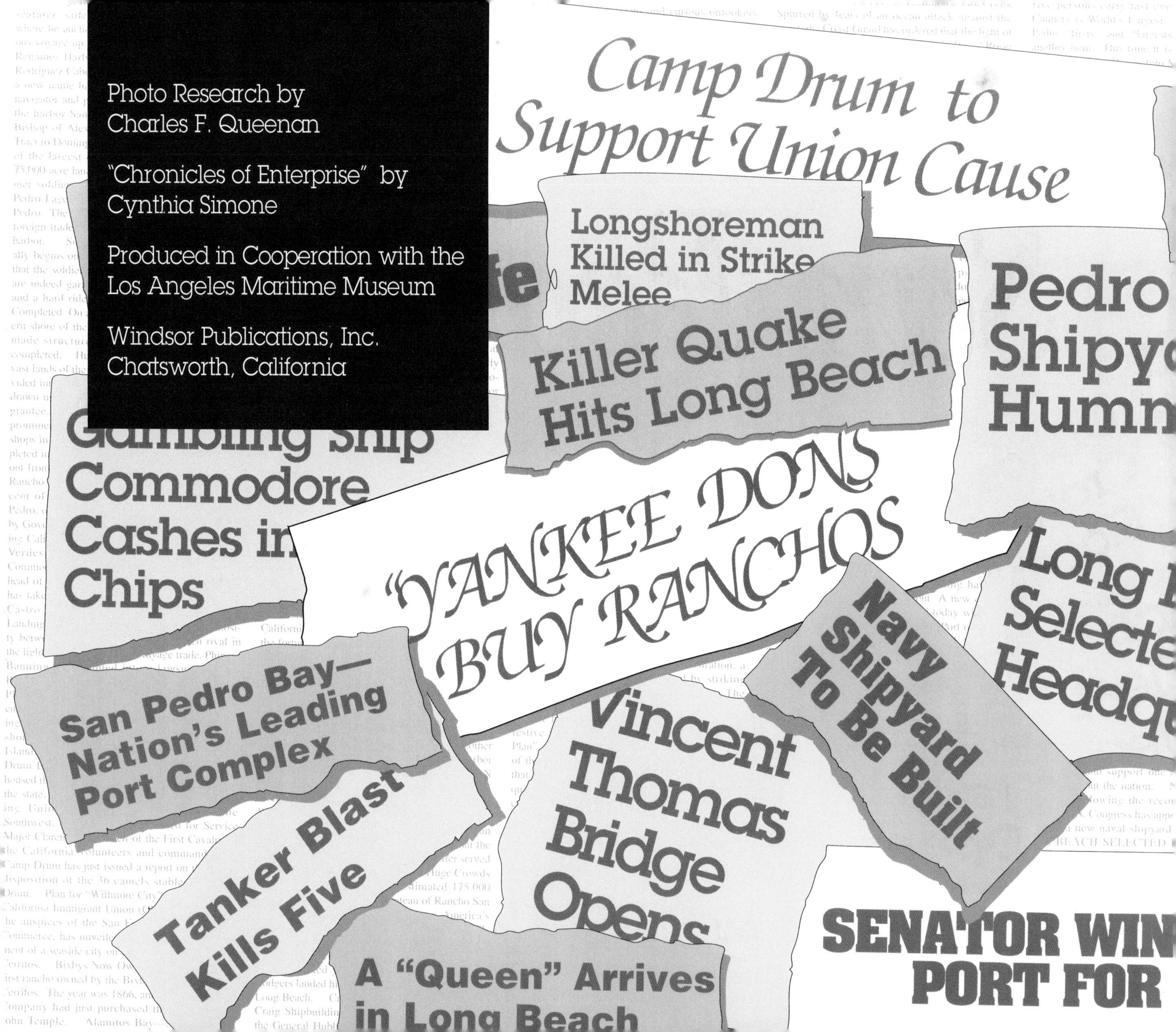

Camp Drum to
Support Union Cause

Longshoreman
Killed in Strike
Melee

Killer Quake
Hits Long Beach

Pedro
Shipy...
Humn...

Gambling Ship
Commodore
Cashes in
Chips

"YANKEE DONS
BUY RANCHOS"

Long...
Selecte...
Headqu...

San Pedro Bay—
Nation's Leading
Port Complex

Navy
Shipyard
To Be Built

Vincent
Thomas
Bridge
Opens

Tanker Blast
Kills Five

A "Queen" Arrives
in Long Beach

SENATOR WIN...
PORT FOR...

Headlines in History

San Pedro Bay Area

featuring
Long Beach, San Pedro,
and Wilmington

by Stephen T. Sato

With thanks to my mother Hazel, Sam, Reiko, Pete and Arlene, and Barry . . . all of whom simultaneously encouraged, supported, and prodded me throughout the project

Windsor Publications, Inc.—History Book Division
Managing Editor: Karen Story
Design Director: Alexander D'Anca
Photo Director: Susan L. Wells
Executive Editor: Pamela Schroeder

Staff for *San Pedro Bay Area*
Editorial Director: Teri Davis Greenberg
Senior Editor, Chronicles of Enterprise: Judith L. Hunter
Production Editor, Chronicles of Enterprise: Doreen Nakakihara
Proofreader: Mary Jo Scharf
Customer Service Manager: Phyllis Feldman-Schroeder
Editorial Assistants: Kim Kievman, Michael Nugwynne, Kathy B.
    Peyser, Theresa J. Solis
Publisher's Representative, Chronicles of Enterprise: Todd
    Indermuehle
Editorial Layout Artists: Alex D'Anca, Bonnie Felt, S. L. Wells
Layout Artist, Chronicles of Enterprise: Lisa Barrett

Windsor Publications, Inc.
Elliot Martin, Chairman of the Board
James L. Fish III, Chief Operating Officer
Paul Pender, Vice President/Sales
Mac Buhler, Vice President/Sponsor Acquisitions

Library of Congress Cataloging-in Publication Data
Sato, Stephen T.
    San Pedro bay area : featuring Long Beach, San Pedro, and
    Wilmington / by Stephen T. Sato ; photo research by Charles F.
    Queenan ; chronicles of enterprise by Cynthia Simone.
        p.   cm — (Headlines in history)
    "Produced in cooperation with the Los Angeles Maritime
    Museum."
    Includes bibliographic references and index.
    ISBN 0-89781-350-2 (alk. paper)
    1. San Pedro (Los Angeles, Calif.) — History. 2. San Pedro (Los
Angeles, Calif.)—Description—Views. 3. San Pedro (Los Angeles,
Calif.)—Industries. 4. Long Beach (Calif.)—History. 5. Long
Beach (Calif.) —Description—Views. 6. Long Beach (Calif.)—
Industries. 7. Wilmington (Los Angeles, Calif.)—History.
8. Wilmington (Los Angeles, Calif.)—Description—Views.
9. Wilmington (Los Angeles, Calif.)—Industries. 10. Los Angeles
(Calif.)—History. I Los Angeles Maritime Museum. II Title
III. Series.
F868.L86S267 1990
979.4'94—dc20   90-38216
                                                                          CIP
                                                                          AC

Contents

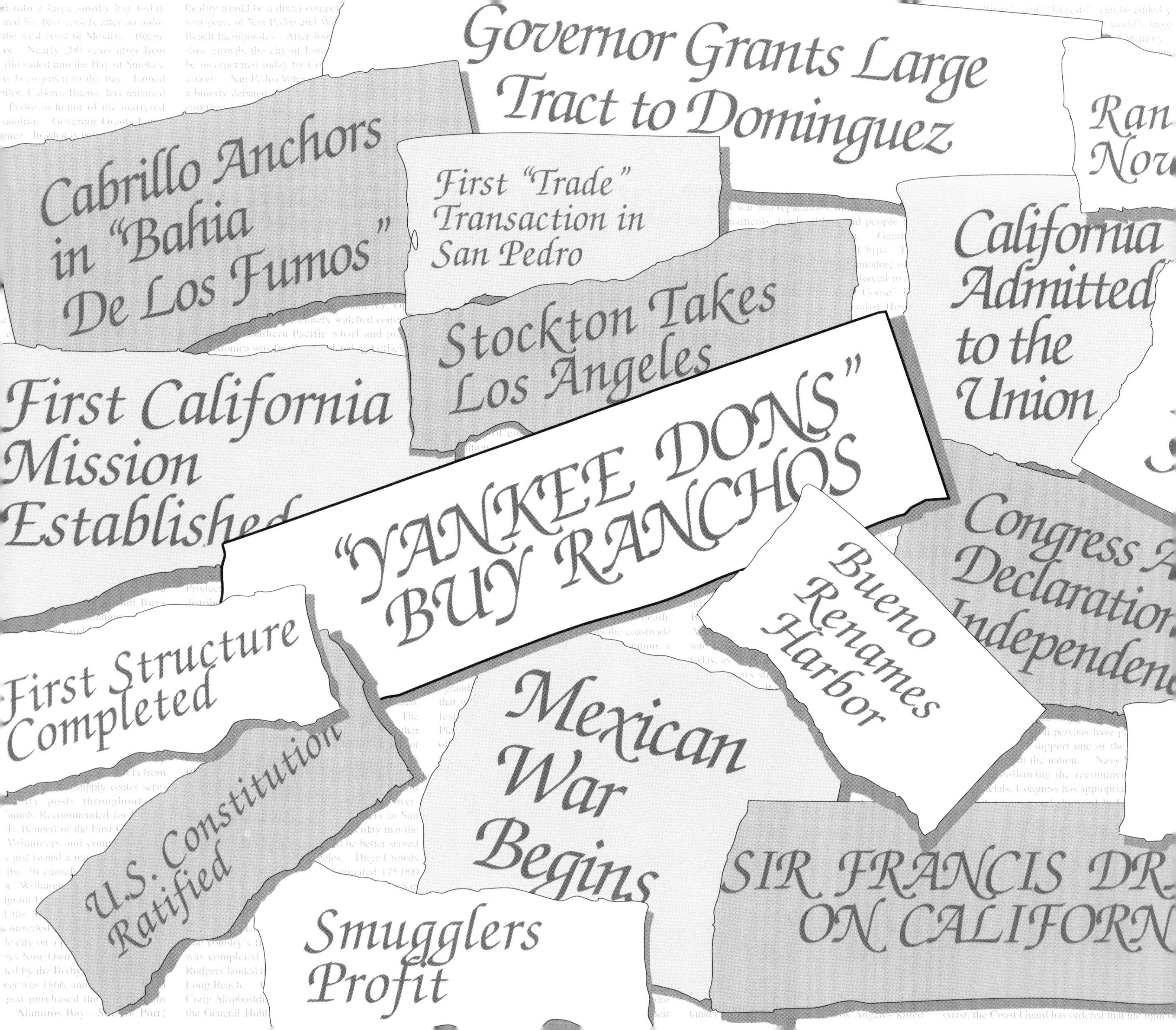

Governor Grants Large Tract to Dominguez

Ran
Nou

Cabrillo Anchors in "Bahia De Los Fumos"

First "Trade" Transaction in San Pedro

California Admitted to the Union

First California Mission Established

Stockton Takes Los Angeles

"YANKEE DONS" BUY RANCHOS

Congress
Declaration
Independen

First Structure Completed

U.S. Constitution Ratified

Mexican War Begins

Bueno Renames Harbor

Smugglers Profit

SIR FRANCIS DR
ON CALIFORN

Exploration and Settlement

(1542-1850)

Cabrillo Anchors in "Bahia de Los Fumos"

(1542, October 8) Juan Rodriguez Cabrillo, Portuguese explorer and seafarer, sailed into a large smokey bay today where he anchored his two vessels after an arduous voyage up the west coast of Mexico. A fine haze covered most of the shoreline, and Cabrillo and his crew immediately named the bay "Bahia de los Fumos," the Bay of Smokes. The explorer believes that the smoke is a result of fires set by the natives to scare up game during hunts.

Cabrillo related that his small, broad-bowed caravels had an especially difficult time during the last three months of the journey. "We experienced strong headwinds and rough seas that were almost unrelenting," said the explorer.

The expedition was commissioned by the viceroy of New Spain, Don Antonio de Mendoza. The stated mission was to discover the long-sought shortcut to Cathay via a northwest route or passage. Cabrillo and his vessels, the flagship *San Salvador* (which is owned by the seaman) and the *La Vittoria,* departed Navidad in June of this year.

Cabrillo's first landfall in Alta California was a fine, natural harbor about 120 miles south of the Bay of Smokes. Cabrillo reported that a fishing party that he sent ashore was attacked by the natives, and three of his men were injured. The expedition claimed the harbor and its surrounding lands for the Spanish Crown and then proceeded north.

After another week's sailing, the ships came into sighting of two islands. These two islands were named for the two ships of the voyage. The explorer spent only one day at the islands, during which time he exchanged gifts with the natives.

The following morning found the voyagers gazing curiously at the shoreline of what some of them believed to be another island. Estimating that this other island was only about 20 miles from their present site, Cabrillo then decided to set out for this unknown land mass.

Upon anchoring at the bay, the men discovered that this was an excellent natural harbor for ships. Cabrillo, as captain of the enterprise, commented at how the high peninsula on the north

While searching for a shortcut to Cathay, Portuguese explorer Juan Rodriguez Cabrillo and his crew have anchored their caravels briefly in the bay they have named Bahia de los Fumos.

side of the crescent-shaped bay offered protection from the prevailing northwest winds. However, the mariners did note the presence of a small island that might present a hazard to future visitors to the bay. This island, about a half mile from shore, is about 50 feet in height and about 2 acres in area.

The sailors also noted a long, narrow bar of sand dunes that extended from west to east at the inner portion of the bay. This bar also afforded protection to the mud sloughs and swamps that lay on the inner shoreline.

Cabrillo and his crew will remain at the Bay of Smokes for only one day. Tomorrow the expedition will continue its northward journey along the coast in its search for the passage to Cathay.

Bueno Renames Harbor

(1734) Nearly 200 years after Juan Rodriguez Cabrillo sailed into the Bay of Smokes, a new name has been given to the bay. Famed navigator and pilot, Cabrero Bueno, has renamed the harbor San Pedro in honor of the martyred Bishop of Alexandria, Saint Peter, who was killed in the year A.D. 311.

When Sebastian Vizcaino passed through the area in 1602, the navigation charts still listed the harbor as the Bay of Smokes. Vizcaino was on a mission to locate and establish ports for the Spanish government for its trading vessels traveling from the Philippines

to Spain. He arrived at the bay on November 26, 1602, and named it Ensenada de San Andres, mistakenly believing the day to be the feast day of that saint.

Bueno is on a similar mission to that of Vizcaino; the navigator was commissioned to lay out new routes for the Spanish galleons that are crossing the Pacific Ocean from the Philippine Islands with their goods destined for the storehouses of Spanish merchants.

Governor Grants Large Tract to Dominguez

(1784) In what is believed to be one of the largest of its kind in Alta California, a 75,000-acre land grant has been awarded to a former soldier of the Spanish Army by Governor Pedro Fages.

Juan Jose Dominguez, a 65-year-old veteran, was granted title to the huge tract of land in appreciation and recognition of his service to the Spanish Crown. Dominguez served in the 1769 expedition of colonization and occupation of Alta California led by Gaspar de Portola.

The land area of the grant encompasses all of the Palos Verdes Peninsula and stretches to the San Gabriel River to the east. To the north it extends to the area several miles north of Palos Verdes and to the south it reaches all the way to the shores of San Pedro.

Although several others have been granted lands for sacrifices and hardships endured during their military careers, Dominguez' is believed to be one of the largest on record.

Dominguez, who has said he will name his holding Rancho San Pedro, is planning to build a house in the hills located about eight miles from the ocean. Situated near the flood plain of the San Gabriel River, he plans to raise corn in these rich lands. With the large amount of land available to the rancho, a considerable cattle ranch will also be a part of the huge grant.

During his service in the Portola expedition, Dominguez served under a young lieutenant, a certain Pedro Fages. Thus, it was to his former commander, and now, military governor, that Dominguez petitioned for the land grant.

First "Trade" Transaction in San Pedro

(1805) The first exchange of goods with a foreign trader was completed today in San Pedro harbor.

The vessel *Lelia Byrd,* sailing out of New England and captained by one William Shaler, off-loaded quantities of cloth, sugar, tools, and utensils to awaiting carts and wagons. In return, the crew of the ship took on otter pelts, cattle hides, and ship's stores.

Although unconfirmed, there are reports that the traders in San Pedro were padres and others from the Mission San Gabriel.

San Pedro is home to an abundance of sea otters, and the otter pelts have become valuable items of barter in recent years. Russian seamen are known to have ventured over the northern expanses of the Pacific Ocean to hunt the furry sea animals in the northern sections of the coast.

Since the end of the Americans' victory over England in the colonists' war of independence, commerce across the Atlantic has been closed to the "Yankee Trader." Seeking new outlets for their products, more and more trading vessels out of Boston and other ports in New England have been seen along the coast of Alta California. So alarming has the situation become, that Governor Pedro Fages recently proclaimed that all foreign vessels are forbidden to enter ports in California. The only exceptions to this edict are ships in desperate need of repairs or supplies.

One of the crewmen on the *Lelia Byrd,* who insisted on not giving his name, said that two years ago Captain Shaler and the crew barely escaped with their lives in San Diego. After picking up a load of confiscated otter skins, their vessel came under heavy cannon fire from Fort Guijarro as they were attempting to leave the harbor.

When asked about this first-ever endeavor, Captain Shaler only indicated that he felt that it was beneficial to both sides of the transaction, and that it was possible that more such exchanges could be had in the future.

SMUGGLERS PROFIT

(This article is compiled from exclusive confidential interviews)

(1815) The operation usually begins only after the ship's master is assured that the soldiers from the Pueblo de Los Angeles are indeed garrisoned at the post some 20 miles and a hard ride from the port. Then, if the winds are right, the transit is swift across the channel between Catalina Island and the mainland at San Pedro Bay. Upon anchoring in the bay, the operation now moves in earnest.

Loading ready-made shoes, utensils, tools, clothing, and even some luxury items into small rowboats, the crew works quickly, preparing to take its precious goods to shore. There crewmen will be met by residents of missions in the area, most notably, those from the Mission San Gabriel, as well as rancheros from nearby ranchos.

On a recent day, when such activities were being viewed from a vantage point on the bluff above the shore, a padre, requesting to remain anonymous, justified the mission padres'

actions. "You must remember, our lives here in Alta California are harsh, to say the least. We are in need of at least a minimum of comforts with which we are accustomed; it makes our witness to the natives here that much more effective."

It is a well-known fact that there exists deep dissatisfaction with the policies of Spain's House of Trade as they apply to the residents of Alta California. The two ships that call at the port annually bring only such goods that are deemed necessary for the padres and government officials and other Spanish subjects living in the area. Luxury items and other amenities usually are not in the shipments.

After unloading the goods and carrying them up the embankment, the crew reverses the process . . . this time with the items for which the risky venture is really undertaken.

Cattle hides from the large ranchos of San Pedro, Verdugo, and Nieto, together with sea otter pelts and supplies for the ship, are taken back to the waiting vessel. Then begins the second voyage across the channel to anchor on the leeward side of the island.

The cost of each otter pelt ranges from one to five dollars; an enterprising ship captain can sell the same pelt for $500 in China, where otter pelts are coveted by the officials of the empire. The cattle hides are likewise in great demand by the American industries in the northeastern part of the new country. There they are used to manufacture shoes and to make the belts needed for operating machinery.

One Spanish official who was interviewed said that many of the government's representatives sympathize with, if not outrightly condone, the actions of the local traders. "After all," said the official, "we too must live here; we are no different than the padres and the rancheros."

First Structure Completed

(1823) On a bluff overlooking the southwestern shore of the bay of San Pedro, the first man-made structure in the harbor area has been completed.

A small, one-room adobe collection and storage house has been built to further the area's trade in hides and tallow. Built by the mission fathers of San Gabriel in the embarcadero section of the hundred varas area of the shoreline, the house will be used to store hides and tallow before loading them onto waiting ships.

The construction was under the supervision of one William Logan. The structure itself is owned by two British traders in the Pueblo de Los Angeles, William Hartnell and Andrew McCulloch.

Last year, after Mexico's independence from Spain and the resulting liberalization of trade with foreign nations, Hartnell and McCulloch entered into a trading contract with most of the missions. The agreement stated that the two traders would provide luxury and ready-made goods to the mission staff in exchange for cattle hides, tallow, and the ever-popular otter pelts.

The hides will be pushed over the bluff above the bay onto the shore below. From there, crewmen of the

trading ships will have to carry the hides to small boats that will then be rowed to the waiting ships anchored offshore.

The reverse process of bringing the manufactured goods on shore will, of course, pose much greater problems. After off-loading the goods onto the shore, the crewmen will have to carry the items on their backs up the steep incline to the adobe storage house.

The trade in hides and tallow has grown quickly due to the demand for leather in the shoe industry in the American northeastern states. So common and valuable has this commodity become that some of the traders have taken to calling the hides "California banknotes."

Huge Nieto Lands Subdivided

(1833) The vast lands of the Nieto land grant have been subdivided into five smaller parcels according to a plan drawn up by Juan Jose Nieto, son of the original grantee.

The heirs of Manuel Perez Nieto have been petitioning for several years for a division of the lands. Juan Jose's plan calls for the creation of five new ranchos. These are to be called Los Cerritos, Los Alamitos, Los Bolsas,

Los Coyotes, and Santa Gertrudes. Nieto said that he plans to retain control of Los Coyotes and Los Alamitos.

The original land grant was made to the elder Nieto in 1784 by Governor Pedro Fages in appreciation for the service that Nieto rendered as a member of the Portola expedition of 1769. It was at the same time that two other Portola veterans, Juan Jose Dominguez and Jose Maria Verdugo were also given land grants by the Spanish Crown.

Nieto's grant was, by far, the largest, covering 300,000 acres. Its boundaries extended from the El Camino Real on the north to the ocean and from the San Gabriel River on the west to the Santa Ana River on the east.

The lands subdivided by Nieto's

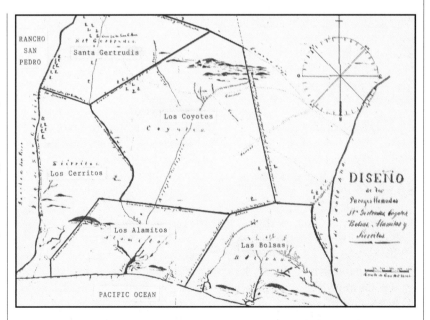

Juan Jose Nieto has subdivided his father's vast holdings into five smaller parcels.

son, however, were barely half of the original grant. A long-running dispute over the alleged grazing of Nieto cattle on Indian-owned lands resulted in the family forfeiting a large parcel of land in the San Gabriel Valley. Today the Nieto lands comprise 170,000 acres.

"Yankee Dons" Buy Ranchos

(1843) Two prominent businessmen with thriving mercantile shops in the Pueblo de Los Angeles recently completed individual purchases of two ranchos carved out from the large rancho of Manuel Perez Nieto.

Abel Stearns, formerly of Massachusetts, bought the Rancho Los Alamitos as a summer home for him and his wife, the former Dona Arcadia Bandini, one of the daughters of the well-known Don Juan Bandini. The purchase was made from the estate of former Governor Figueroa for $6,000 in goods.

Soon after, John Temple and his wife, Doña Rafaela Cota, second cousin by marriage to Manuela Nieto de Cota and heiress to the Rancho Los Cerritos, bought the rancho for $3,025 from Manuela's heirs.

As only Mexican citizens can hold property in California, both men became citizens of Mexico early on in their careers. Stearns has been a Catholic since his youth in Massachusetts, and Temple adopted the religion after gaining his Mexican citizenship. The choice of religion certainly does not work against them in their business and real estate dealings. The term "Yankee Don" has been ascribed to such businessmen who, seeing great opportunity in California, are willing to change their citizenship (and their religion in some cases) and marry the daughters of prominent Mexican families.

With the purchases of the two ranchos, it seems as if the "Yankee Dons" are indeed reaping the benefits of what they have sown.

Former Massachusetts resident Abel Stearns has purchased the Rancho Los Alamitos for $6,000 in goods.

For $3,025, "Yankee Don" John Temple has become the owner of Rancho Los Cerritos.

Rancho Palos Verdes Now Official

(1846) Nearly 40 percent of the Dominguez family's Rancho San Pedro, or 31,000 acres, was officially ceded today by Governor Pio Pico to the Sepulveda clan, creating California's newest rancho, the Rancho Palos Verdes.

The Sepulveda rancho encompasses all of the city of San Pedro, the high bluffs and peninsula to the northwest, and the surrounding flatland areas. The government action culminates nearly four decades of bitter arguments between the area's two most powerful families.

The Dominguez holding was one of the first major ranchos established by the Spanish Crown in 1784. After the death of the Dominguez patriarch and original grantee, Juan Jose Dominguez, his nephew, Sergeant Cristobal Dominguez, was named as heir of the rancho as dictated by Juan Jose's will. However, because of his assignment as Commander of the Guard at Mission San Juan Capistrano, Cristobal could not be physically present to direct the affairs of the huge, sprawling rancho. These duties acceded to Manuel Gutierrez, Juan Jose's executor and head steward.

It was at this point that the long-running feud with the Sepulvedas had its birth.

Jose Dolores Sepulveda, then a young Spanish officer, was assigned as the commander of the garrison at the Pueblo de Los Angeles in 1822. After befriending Gutierrez, Sepulveda obtained permission to graze his herds of cattle and horses on the Palos Verdes Peninsula area of the Rancho San Pedro.

Cristobal, upon learning of this use of his property, protested vehemently to the Sepulvedas to no avail. Then, in a bold and aggressive move, Jose Dolores laid claim to the area that he was occupying as well as a large portion of the Dominguez rancho and named it Rancho Los Palos Verdes.

Later, armed with government edicts, Cristobal repeatedly pressed his demand for the Sepulvedas to vacate the Palos Verdes area of the rancho. Again, these efforts were in vain as the occupants resolutely continued to press their claim as owners of Rancho Palos Verdes.

In 1824, upon returning from a meeting with Governor Pico in Monterey, at

Right: Nearly 25 years after Jose Dolores Sepulveda grazed his cattle on the Rancho San Pedro without the consent of the rancho's owner, the governor has officially ceded 40 percent of the land of Sepulveda's heirs.

which he pressed his claim to the Palos Verdes rancho, Jose Dolores was killed by natives in an uprising at the Mission de la Purisima Concepcion. The death did not deter the Sepulveda heirs, and they continued in their demands to the governor. In 1827 a provisional grant to Rancho Palos Verdes was given to Jose Dolores' heirs, the oldest child at the time being only 10 years of age.

Now, nearly 20 years after that 1827 grant, the official grant from Governor Pico has been made to two of Jose Dolores' sons, Jose Loreto and Juan Sepulveda. Rancho Palos Verdes is now a reality.

Stockton Takes Los Angeles

(1846, August 13) Commodore Robert F. Stockton, newly appointed head of the American naval forces in the Pacific, has taken Los Angeles from General Jose Maria Castro and Governor Pio Pico.

Stockton and 360 men landed in San Pedro on the 56-gun warship, *Congress,* on August 6. The commodore was responsible for an overland effort to engage Castro's troops, while Captain John C. Fremont was assigned to San Diego to halt a southward move by the Californians.

Castro and Pico transferred their defense of California to Los Angeles after the so-called Bear Flag Revolt in Sonoma in June, which was supported by Fremont's detachment. Soon after this, Commodore John Sloat, then commander of the Pacific Naval force, ordered the American flag hoisted

Today, without any bloodshed, Commodore Robert F. Stockton took Los Angeles out of the hands of the Mexican government.

above the government Customs House in Monterey, thereby establishing the official American presence in California.

Claiming that he had only 100 men to defend the garrison in Los Angeles, Castro sought a truce upon the landing of Stockton in San Pedro. The commodore insisted, however, on an unconditional surrender that included the promise of the Californians to declare their independence from Mexico and seek the protection of the Americans. Having no room to negotiate, the Mexican commander gave notice to Stockton that the Californians would fight rather than capitulate. In reality, Castro quickly disbanded his troops, spiked 4 of his 10 cannon, buried the remaining 6, and, together with Governor Pico, fled to Sonora.

Thus, when Stockton and his men marched into Los Angeles today (accompanied by a brass band), the city was taken without a single shot being fired.

With Governor Pico and the chief military leader now departed, the government of Mexico is no longer a force in California.

Rattlesnake Island is now Terminal Island

Timm Buys Landing; Banning Sues

Plan for "Willmore City" Revealed

Banning Builds "New San Pedro'

Bixbys Purchase Second Ranch

Huntington and S.P. Open Port Los Angeles

Camp Drum to Support Union Cause

Feds Ag Deep-Wa at San P

International Port at San Pedro?

Long Beach Incorporates

Finally, Long Bea Reincorporates

Alamitos Bay— Site for Port?

SENATOR WINS PORT FOR S

Federal

Cities and Ports

(1850s-1900)

Timm Buys Landing; Banning Sues

(circa 1855) The continuing animosity between Augustus Timm and his arch rival in the lightering and stage and drayage trade, Phineas Banning, has erupted into a lawsuit filed by Banning.

The issue this time is the purchase of the Sepulveda Landing by Timm. In recently filed court documents, Banning alleges that he was given the right to buy the property from Diego Sepulveda if it ever came up for sale. Banning claims that Timm circumvented that agreement and bought the landing without giving Banning notice of the proposed sale.

Timm, a Prussian immigrant, has been in the San Pedro area for approximately five years. After living near San Francisco and then on Catalina Island, Timm settled on a spot of land adjacent to the Sepulveda Landing, which is located below the San Pedro bluffs and slightly to the north of Deadman's Island.

Salvaging the house and part of the hull of the shipwrecked *Mary Jane,* Timm dragged the pieces onto his land and began using them for living quarters in 1852. Later, the Army cargo carrier *Abraham Lincoln* went aground near Timm's property, and he set to work again. Part of the *Lincoln* was moved next to the previous wreck.

The result of these patchwork quarters was the buildup of sand and silt around the structures. Soon, enough silt had gathered to allow Timm to begin operations as a landing, which he called Timm's Point. It soon was the major point of shipping in the harbor. He then began a stage line to Los Angeles to move the products and passengers inland.

It was about this time that Banning arrived in San Pedro and began to operate a similar business. The men, being strong-willed and independent, each assert that they are the rightful owner of the old Sepulveda Landing. Now it will be in the hands of justice to make the final decision. In the meantime Timm has changed the name of the Sepulveda property to Timm's Landing.

The Sepulveda Landing is the focus of a lawsuit filed by Phineas Banning against Augustus Timm.

Banning Builds "New San Pedro"

(1858) Phineas Banning, the young, energetic entrepreneur out of Delaware, celebrated the opening of his newest endeavor—the new port on the shores of the sloughs in back of Rattlesnake Island.

The new port, called New San Pedro, stands in direct competition with the older port at San Pedro. Banning believes that the fact that his port is four to five miles closer to Los Angeles will attract most of the shipping business in lumber, hides, tallow, grapes, and whale oil away from San Pedro.

New San Pedro is located on 2,400 acres of former Rancho San Pedro land. Banning and two of his partners bought the property for $12,000 from the Dominguez family in 1854 and began construction in 1857.

The shallow waters of the sloughs should pose no problems for the Banning enterprise. Intercoastal steamers with shallow drafts can operate in the inner harbor and will be able to navigate easily to the docks of New San Pedro. Banning himself has indicated that he will soon build his own fleet of flat-bottomed barges and shallow draft steamers to ferry people and cargo to and from waiting ships.

Ever since his arrival in San Pedro in 1851, Banning has been a force to be reckoned with in the drayage and transportation business. Starting by rowing water and supplies to ships at anchor, Banning soon moved into the stagecoach and cargo-hauling business by buying John Temple's share of the Temple and Alexander transportation company. Within five years Banning's aggressive business sense increased the company's rolling stock to 15 stages and 50 drayage wagons. By obtaining lucrative government contracts, the firm soon was serving military outposts in Utah, Arizona, Texas, New Mexico, and California.

When a spring storm destroyed Banning's small wharf on Timm's Landing last year, he and his partners decided that the time was right for the brand-new enterprise at New San Pedro. In a further effort to establish an identity separate from San Pedro, Banning is already planning to rename the new port after his hometown in Delaware—Wilmington.

Camp Drum will soon supply Union military posts throughout the Southwest.

Camp Drum to Support Union Cause

(1862) Drum Barracks, a new Army post that initially housed the "California Column," volunteers from the state, will soon become a supply center serving Union military posts throughout the Southwest.

The California Volunteers were recently assigned to posts in Arizona and New Mexico to secure these territories for the Union cause.

The barracks had their genesis three years ago when Lieutenant Winfield Scott Hancock was given the task of obtaining land on which to build a post for the Army Quartermaster's Department of the Southwest.

For consideration of one dollar, Phineas Banning, an ardent supporter of the Union cause, and his partner, Benjamin David Wilson, donated 60 acres for the future site of the barracks. In return, Banning and Wilson were granted all of the contracts for the construction of the installation and were paid to build a flume to transport water from the San Gabriel River to Drum Barracks.

In addition to its quartermaster functions, the post will also serve as a base of operations against southwestern Indian tribes. As such, Drum Barracks is equipped with a modern telegraph system that links it with sev-

eral other federal installations in the region.

Consisting of 20 buildings, the site is made up of a 30-acre headquarters section, officers' quarters, the adjutant's office, five enlisted barracks, bakery, granary, barn, blacksmith and wheelwright shops, hospital, four laundry buildings, a guard house, and a powder magazine. Additionally, depot and commissary buildings are located on seven acres of land near the Banning landing in Wilmington.

The barracks are named for Adjutant General Richard Coulter Drum, the head of the Army's Department of the West.

This army camel, one of 36 stabled at Camp Drum, was photographed at Canal and Front streets in Wilmington.

Camels Recommended for Desert Service

(1863) Major Clarence E. Bennett of the First Cavalry of the California Volunteers and commandant of Camp Drum has just issued a report on the future disposition of the 36 camels stabled at Camp Drum.

Citing the rapid depletion of surrounding forage, Bennett advocates transferring the animals to San Bernardino where food supplies are much more plentiful. From there they should be trained for service in the Mojave Desert.

The contingent of camels came to Camp Drum two years ago from their former station at Fort Tejon, north of Los Angeles. They have been kept at the camp near the Banning Wharf ever since their arrival in Wilmington.

The Camel Corps experiment began in 1856 when Jefferson Davis, then Secretary of War, persuaded Congress to allocate $30,000 for the purchase of camels to be used in the arid Southwest. Reports of the successful use of the animals in the Crimean War were convincing factors in the decision. It was said that the British and their allies used 8,000 camels for transportation and cavalry purposes.

Dispatched to the Mediterranean were two early advocates of the Camel Corps, Major Henry C. Wayne and Lieutenant David D. Porter. Both men had studied the animals extensively before their departure and were shrewd buyers upon their arrival in the Middle East.

The first group of 33 camels was purchased by the two officers for $250 per camel. The "ships of the desert" were off-loaded at Indianola, Texas, and then later moved to Camp Verde, some 60 miles northwest of San Antonio. Porter then went back to the Mediterranean for a second purchase.

One of Major Wayne's first jobs once the animals arrived was to educate the skeptical mule skinners and packers who would be working with the camels. Although several handlers were hired to accompany the camels, the strange animals were distrusted and outrightly despised by the Americans.

The unfamiliar appearance and strong smell of the animals scares and disrupts the mules and horses of a pack train. And, though highly domesticated in the Mideast and Asia, the camels are often treated harshly by the mule skinners. The common mode of defense against this mistreatment is the spitting of a malodorous wad of cud at the handlers, which only intensifies their hatred of the animals.

One of the first converts of Major Wayne was Lieutenant Edward F. Beale. An adventurous type who joined the Navy at 14 and later served with Kit Carson during the Mexican-American War, Beale was personally persuaded to join the Camel Corps experiment by Wayne himself.

After several months of familiarization of the habits and care of camels, Beale was assigned to chart a new route from Fort Defiance on the Arizona-New Mexico border to Fort Tejon on the western edge of the Mojave Desert.

Selecting 25 of the best camels, Beale left Fort Defiance with 10 mule-drawn wagons and a 55-man company of cooks, surveyors, handlers, mule drivers, and cavalry. During the journey Beale made several careful observations of the camels' performance. He noted that three camels could carry as much as six mules pulling a wagon, that they could swim and ford a river when horses and mules could not, and that they were adaptable to higher elevations and colder climates.

Beale conducted several more expeditions with camels, one from Fort Smith, Arkansas, to Fort Defiance and another from Fort Tejon back to Defiance. All of these journeys were supplemented by glowing reports of the performance of the camels.

With the rumblings of the present civil conflict on the horizon, Beale was reassigned to the East, and the camels at Fort Tejon were transferred to Los Angeles by Colonel Carleton and a contingent of dragoons who were assigned to the city when war was declared.

Plan for "Willmore City" Revealed

(1880) The California Immigrant Union (CIU), formed under the auspices of the San Francisco Chamber of Commerce, has unveiled a plan for the development of a seaside city on a portion of Rancho Los Cerritos.

The 10,000-acre site, designed by the manager of the CIU's southern division, William E. Willmore, was initially called the "American Colony" by its chief proponent, Willmore. However, the colony has come to be known as Willmore City because of the personal involvement of its namesake.

The CIU was created in 1870 by the San Francisco Chamber with the express purpose of encouraging families to move to California. Many business and civic leaders believe that the solid foundation provided by the families will give California communities the necessary foundations to grow into respectable and stable cities.

Willmore was successful in an earlier CIU project. He was sent to the Central Valley to start a community of teachers interested in growing raisin grapes. This colony calls itself Fresno. Other projects that the CIU has sponsored have resulted in the births of the cities of Pasadena and Riverside.

In order to design his city, Willmore

first needed to convince Jotham Bixby to subdivide part of his rancho for the future community. Bixby, an ardent supporter of the goals of the CIU and one its major subscribers, readily agreed to the action and gave the American Colony his blessing.

Willmore's plan calls for a small town with wide streets, churches, schools, parks, a city hall, a boardwalk, hotels overlooking the ocean, and a college. Farming will be the principal activity of the new city and will support its activities. In order to stimulate sales in the colony, lots will be sold for only $25 an acre.

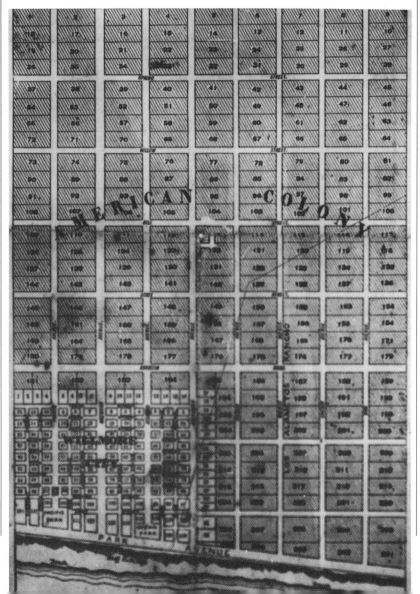

The American Colony Tract, a plat of which is seen here, is subdivided into 5, 10, and 20-acre parcels priced from $50 to $75 per acre.

Bixbys Purchase Second Rancho

(1881) The first rancho owned by the Bixbys was Rancho Los Cerritos. The year was 1866, and Flint, Bixby and Company had just purchased the rancho from John Temple for the sum of $20,000. And now a second rancho has been added to the Bixby family empire. John Bixby, cousin of Jotham Bixby, has just purchased Rancho Los Alamitos from the Michael Reese estate for $125,000. Bixby's partners in this transaction were J. Bixby and Company and I.W. Hellman, a prominent Los Angeles banker.

Temple, like others at the time, was experiencing harsh economic conditions due to the vagaries of weather that hit the area during the early 1860s.

The torrential rains of the winter of 1861-1862, followed by a drought later that summer, spelled the beginning of financial setbacks for Temple. Thus, in 1866, the once-powerful Don Juan, after losing thousands of head of cattle, sold his land to the Flint-Bixby family and moved to San Francisco. He died there several years later.

Abel Stearns, a neighbor of Temple's and owner of Rancho Los Alamitos, fared no better during the harsh times of the 1860s. Reports from the time say that Stearns lost more than 50,000 head of cattle on his rancho due to the droughts of the period.

Overextended and delinquent on his tax payments, Stearns mortgaged his rancho to San Franciscan

Michael Reese in 1861. Then, unable to meet the payments, Stearns lost the rancho outright to Reese in 1866. Five years later Stearns also passed on, thus bringing an end to a colorful and important part of the development of this area south of Los Angeles.

With the acquisition of Los Alamitos, the Bixby-Flint family clan is now the largest landholder of waterfront property on the San Pedro Bay.

Jotham Bixby was co-founder of the family dynasty that purchased Rancho Los Cerritos in 1866 and Rancho Los Alamitos recently.

Alamitos Bay—Site for Port?

(1886) Alamitos Bay has been suggested as a site for a port to serve the Los Angeles area. The new cargo facility would be a direct competitor with the present ports of San Pedro and Wilmington on the west side of the San Pedro Bay.

The bold plan was recently unveiled by one of Long Beach's leading citizens, John Bixby, part owner of Rancho Los Alamitos. The proposal for the new port is part of a larger plan that Bixby has for a planned colony to be located east of Long Beach. Bixby believes that the city will expand eastward, and his port would then be in an ideal location to serve the entire county.

Alamitos Bay has, in the past, been a cargo port for hides and tallow, the two commodities that gave both San Pedro and Wilmington their starts as shipping centers.

Already, General Barton has been in contact with the Atchison, Topeka, and Santa Fe Railroad, seeking to convince it to build a line linking Long Beach and Los Angeles. Barton has also obtained approval for a railroad right-of-way along Second Street.

Barton, for his efforts, would obtain choice lands at the port area from Bixby. These areas would then be developed as wharves, piers, and a railyard terminal.

Long Beach Incorporates

(1888, February 10) After four years of painfully slow growth, Long Beach will finally be incorporated today by County of Los Angeles action.

Ever since the disastrous "Willmore City" attempt at cityhood failed in 1884, the community has struggled to gain not only businesses, but permanent residents as well.

The city was named "Long Beach" by Belle Lowe a month after William Willmore was forced to give up his attempt to establish a city under the sponsorship of the California Immigrant Union.

Despite the CIU's withdrawal of support for Willmore's project in 1882, he persisted in his efforts to develop his dream city. He desperately contracted with Jotham Bixby to purchase 4,000 acres of the development himself. The terms of repayment called for a $25,000 payment in four months, a second installment of $30,000 in June of 1883, and the final payment in June of 1884.

A hastily called auction in October of 1882 resulted in some sales, but not nearly enough to stave off the

Long Beach, one of the nation's leading resorts, is now officially a city.

impending disaster. In May of 1885, Willmore, unable to pay the notes due Bixby, gave up his long-cherished dream and relinquished his rights to the land. Disillusioned and broken of spirit, Willmore left the city and moved to Arizona.

The Long Beach Water and Land Company now entered the picture, paying Bixby $240,000 for the option to the lands forfeited by Willmore. The company also paid Willmore $8,000 for the water and sewer system that he had installed. It was at this time that the present name of the city was coined.

In 1887 the rights to the unsold portions of the city were purchased by the Long Beach Development Company for $250,000. Some of the individuals in the company are reportedly associated with the Southern Pacific Railroad. As part of the purchase, the company was compelled to take some 800 acres of worthless marshland west of the city and a short distance from the shorefront.

Today's action by the county board of supervisors will allow the city to officially ban gambling and the sale of alcohol (longtime controversial issues among residents) within the city limits.

San Pedro Votes to Become a City

(1888, February 26) After a bitterly debated contest among residents, voters cast their ballots yesterday, approving San Pedro's incorporation as a city. The final tally showed 145 persons in favor of incorporation and 57 voting against the proposal. Upon announcement of the result, bonfires were spontaneously started, balloons were released, and music was heard throughout the night.

The election was spurred by a

On March 1, 1888, San Pedro will officially become an incorporated city.

desire of the residents to determine their own future by moving out from under the control of Wilmington Township. Residents of the new city had been talking for several years about setting up an independent government body for themselves.

Much of the dissatisfaction felt by the voters can be attributed to the fact that San Pedro has recently seen a tremendous growth in its economic health and has surpassed Wilmington as the center of business in the harbor area. The port moved 450,000 tons of cargo last year. The Southern Pacific's rail extension to Timm's Point on the southwestern shore was a great factor in this new prosperity as was the construction of two jetties in the outer harbor.

For many years the Phineas Banning harbor development at Wilmington held sway over the majority of the shipping business that entered San Pedro Bay. Now that the situation has been reversed, the people of San Pedro are anxious to plan and develop their city and harbor independently of Wilmington.

Incorporation papers will be signed tomorrow, and official incorporation will take place on March 1.

International Port at San Pedro?

(1888) The Los Angeles Chamber of Commerce has given its enthusiastic support for the development of an international deep-water port at San Pedro.

The business development group's decision gives additional credence to the overwhelming belief of many shipping and business leaders that San Pedro is the only logical choice for a deep-water port in Southern California.

With the current economic boom bringing more and more people to Los Angeles, these same business leaders also foresee a corresponding growth in commerce. The San Pedro port is a major entry point for lumber into the region and moves more than 450,000 tons of cargo intercoastally. However, there is a desperate need for a deeper facility to handle international shipping. Increasingly, business leaders say that they are losing lucrative international business shipments to other deep-water ports along the coast.

Canned fruits and vegetables from our own state, hams from the Midwest, and cotton from the South are some of the products that could be sent to the Orient if deep-draft vessels were able to berth at San Pedro.

Proponents of the deep-water port idea emphasize the need to have more improvements done in the inner harbor area, specifically, additional dredging to deepen the shipping channels. Also of critical importance is the construction of a protective breakwater across the mouth of the bay.

Feds Agree:
Deep Water Port at San Pedro

(1888) A federal engineering survey team has submitted its report to Congress on the feasibility of building a deep-water port at San Pedro. The recommendation of the study group is one of overwhelming support for the project.

Headed up by Colonel G.H. Mendell of the War Department Board of Engineers, the report took notice of the natural advantages of San Pedro Bay as determining factors in their decision. The protection from prevailing northwesterly winds provided by the Palos Verdes Peninsula makes the bay the ideal location for an international deep-water port. Further, the fact that the depth of the waters off the coast is not too deep makes the construction of a breakwater a less difficult task.

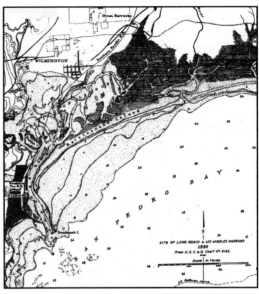

Long Beach and Los Angeles harbors at San Pedro Bay have been recommended as the site for an international deep-water port by a federal engineering survey team.

Should all proceed smoothly, the new breakwater will augment the two existing jetties that the federal government built at Deadman's Island and at Timm's Point.

The U.S. Army Corps of Engineers issued an earlier report in 1880 stating that the two jetties were already responsible for controlling the tidal influences in the inner harbor area. This has resulted in allowing the natural scouring action of the ocean to deepen the harbor channel to 10 feet. The troublesome sandbar at the entrance of the harbor that kept the depth of the water at one and one-half to two feet at that point has also been eliminated because of the two jetties.

Colonel Mendell's recommendation calls for a double-armed breakwater costing $4,045,700. The construction would begin at a point 1,900 feet from the southwestern shoreline and would continue easterly across the mouth of the bay.

Rattlesnake Island is Now Terminal Island

(1891) For as many years as local residents can recall, the spit of land dotted with sand dunes in the inner harbor of the bay was known as Rattlesnake Island. No more. Henceforth the island will be known as Terminal Island.

With the completion of trackage to the western end of the island by the Los Angeles Terminal Railroad, the owners of the company have decided to rename the island to signify the point at which their tracks end.

The island was purchased by a group of St. Louis investors from the Dominguez heirs for $250,000. Then the company promptly formed a corporation to build and operate a new railroad to compete with the Southern Pacific's rail lines into San Pedro on the other side of the channel.

The new railroad's lines run down the eastern side of the Los Angeles River and then across the shallows and mudflats onto the island. Once on the island, the tracks run west to the end of the land. There a new wharf has also been built to attract shippers and ships' captains. So confident are the new railroad operators, that they have also named that portion of the island, "East San Pedro."

Rattlesnake Island was so named by the original Indian inhabitants of the area because of the many snakes that washed ashore on it after winter rains brought them down to the sea via the Los Angeles River.

Rattlesnake Island, seen here across the main channel, will henceforth be called Terminal Island.

Huntington and S.P. Open Port Los Angeles

(1893, July) The closely watched construction of the Southern Pacific wharf and pier at Santa Monica was finally completed and officially opened for cargo vessels. Named "Port Los Angeles" earlier this year, the major undertaking is widely believed to be the result of the personal efforts of Southern Pacific's president, Collis P. Huntington.

The idea for the "Long Wharf" (the length of the wharf is nearly a mile) was hatched several years ago when Huntington announced plans for the shipping facility that would compete with the Port of San Pedro. In 1888, after the release of the Mendell report, which recommended San Pedro as the site for a major deep-water port, the Southern Pacific appeared to be highly supportive of the study team's decision.

The railroad's president at the time, Leland Stanford, even publicly announced that Southern Pacific would build several deep-draft vessels that would be involved in international shipping. In 1890, however, Stanford was forced out of office and replaced by Huntington. Soon after, construction of a Southern Pacific pier in San Pedro was abruptly halted.

In early 1892 the Senate Commerce Committee, chaired by William B. Frye of Maine, began consideration of a $250,000 appropriation for harbor improvements in San Pedro harbor. A letter, purportedly from the Southern Pacific's chief engineer, was introduced by Frye at the hearing. The letter stated that San Pedro's ocean bottom was too rocky to allow piles to be driven into it. Based on this letter, Frye tabled any further action on the appropriation.

A second government study group, this time a five-man team headed by Colonel William Craighill of the War Department's Board of Engineers, was formed to examine the issue once again. The second team again endorsed San Pedro as the site for the deep-water port for Los Angeles. This report was released in December of last year.

Even prior to this time, however, Huntington had quietly started to acquire waterfront property in Santa Monica. Soon the railroad chief accelerated his efforts and before long claimed title to most of Santa Monica's waterfront. Even after Craighill's report was made public, Huntington continued with the construction at Port Los Angeles.

With the completion of the wharf, the Southern Pacific is virtually assured of a total monopoly of the shipping activities at Port Los Angeles. Should the deep-water port be located there and be designated as the official port for Los Angeles, the entire ship-

ping and rail transportation for the region would be controlled by one entity, the Southern Pacific Railroad.

A major obstacle to this scenario, however, is whether or not Congress will authorize federal funds for the construction of a breakwater.

As San Pedro has already been recommended as the site of the deepwater port in Southern California, it remains to be seen whether the government's decision will change because of the new wharf. Huntington is a master power broker and is known for his extensive political influence and access to legislators in Washington. It is certain that he will leave nothing to chance in attempting to establish Port Los Angeles as the only international port serving the city.

On the other side, supporters of the San Pedro site believe that the only way for shippers to obtain fair treatment and rates from the railroad companies is for the tentacles of the oppressive Southern Pacific "Octopus" to be severed once and for all.

The railroad has, over the years, been accused of exorbitant rates and retaliatory practices when dealing with shippers in the area. Many businessmen remember that after the Southern Pacific acquired the Los Angeles & Independence Railroad in Santa Monica in 1877, rates jumped to astounding heights. Because of the absolute control over transportation that the railroad exerted, it soon cost more to ship goods from Los Angeles

Collis P. Huntington's Port Los Angeles in Santa Monica features the "Long Wharf," nearly a mile in length.

to San Pedro than it did to ship the same goods from Hong Kong to San Pedro.

What is certain for now is that the fight for a deep-water port has only just begun, and the eventual outcome may well leave a lasting imprint on the development of the city.

Senator Wins Deep-Water Port for San Pedro

(1896) After a grueling two-day debate on the Senate floor, California Senator Stephen M. White has led what appears to be a successful fight for a deep-water port in San Pedro. Not only is this a significant event for San Pedro, but it also marks one of the rare instances when the Southern Pacific "Octopus" was tied in knots and defeated.

The fight on the full floor of the Senate was part of White's strategy to counter the powerful political machine of the Southern Pacific and its president, Collis P. Huntington.

Earlier in the year the Free Harbor League approached the House Committee on Rivers and Harbors with yet another request for funds to improve San Pedro harbor. Assuming that Huntington would not interfere in this effort, a modest request of only $400,000 was made to dredge the port to a depth of minus 25 feet. Huntington, however, made several unscheduled appearances in front of the Senate Commerce Committee and requested that an additional $3.1 million be added to the appropriation request, and that this amount be allocated for a breakwater at Santa Monica exclusively.

Because of the resulting outcry from the people of Los Angeles over this political maneuvering, which would have funded improvements for competing ports fewer than 20 miles from each other, both items were soon struck from the appropriations list.

The watered-down version of the bill then was passed by the House and forwarded to Senator William Frye's Commerce Committee. There, the $3.1-million request was brazenly restored to the bill and sent to the full Senate for a vote.

Senator White, earlier considered by some to be a disappointment to his backers in the free harbor fight because of his lackluster performance in the Senate, stepped to the forefront and confronted the Southern Pacific almost single-handedly. He introduced an amendment to the River and Harbor Bill that effectively neutralized

Senator Stephen M. White (left) has led a successful fight against Collis P. Huntington (right) and the Southern Pacific Railroad to make San Pedro the site of the deep-water port. Despite several unscheduled appearances before the Senate Commerce Committee, Collis P. Huntington was unable to win support to make Santa Monica the site of the deep-water port.

Huntington's plan for a monopoly at Santa Monica. White proposed that another engineering survey team be sent to Los Angeles to study both of the ports. Whichever site was selected would receive the $3.1 million, and the decision would be a final and binding one. White also stipulated that should Santa Monica be selected, all other railroads would be given the opportunity to operate out of the Long Wharf for a fair and reasonable price.

During the next two days, White staved off all attempts by Senator Frye and Huntington to change his demands. The California senator constantly emphasized the detrimental effect that the selection of Santa

Monica would have on business and international trade should the Southern Pacific be afforded yet another opportunity to create a monopoly on transportation services.

Finally, after the exhausting two-day ordeal was over, the River and Harbor Bill, with White's amendment intact, was passed by both the House and Senate. The bill is now expected to become law in June of this year.

EXTRA ELECTION ISSUE Finally, Long Beach Reincorporates

(1897, December 1) After nearly 10 years of acrimonious debate that many times pitted friend against friend and tore families apart, the issue of city incorporation has finally been resolved. The city's voters today decided to reincorporate Long Beach.

The results of today's election bring to an end a fight that began almost as soon as the City of Long Beach first incorporated in 1888. The underlying, and at times, unspoken, issue at hand was, of course, whether Long Beach would be a "wet" or "dry" city.

The city's first ordinance drew the lines between those favoring libations and those opposing them. This first official action absolutely banned

alcohol sales in the city. Yet, one year later, an amended law allowed for wine to be served in hotels with 15 or more rooms, but only to guests staying there.

"Wets" felt they were making progress with the city council, when, in 1890, a new law opened the city to retail liquor sales, with some restrictions. Sales could not be made to children or to those whom the retailers were requested not to sell by wives, husbands, fathers, mothers, children, and guardians.

Hardly had this system gone into effect, when the "drys" again took hold of the council and once more banned retail liquor sales. For the next six years, it seemed that Long Beach would remain a safe haven for "drys." But the "wets" would not go away

without a fight.

Seeing that their wishes could only be had if the city was taken out of the whims of the city council, the "wets" began circulating a petition for disincorporation of Long Beach. They found a willing ally in other local forces disgruntled by the high city taxes that were being levied.

The vote was held on July 27, 1896, and by a margin of six votes (132-126) disincorporation forces had a victory. Seeking to forestall the action, the city council refused to report the results to the county board of supervisors as required by law.

The state supreme court finally intervened in the conflict and ordered the disincorporation in June of this year.

McCarthy's saloon has been a stronghold for Long Beach's "wets."

The reality and consequences of the vote were not fully felt, however, until the quasi-city started to suffer because of its non-status. City parks, streets, and beach facilities were neglected and allowed to deteriorate. Public street lamps went unrepaired, and county tax levies rose to all-time highs. Finally, out of sheer desperation, a move was made to reincorporate the city.

Today's vote, 237 to 27 in favor of becoming a city once again, reflects the frustration that the past year has wrought on the citizens. Long Beach is once again a city!

FEDERAL BREAKWATER STARTED

(1899, April 27) After 11 years of bitter combat with the formidable machinery of Collis P. Huntington's Southern Pacific Railroad, San Pedro can finally lay claim as the deep-water port of Los Angeles.

Yesterday at 11 a.m. President William McKinley pressed a button in the White House signalling the release of a bargeload of stone into San Pedro Bay. This symbolic first load of stone marked the official start of the construction of the long-awaited federal breakwater at San Pedro.

Twenty thousand people came to the bay to witness the event that some daring business leaders predict will change forever the way that Los Angeles conducts foreign trade. After the laying of the rocks, guests were invited to a huge barbecue celebration at the La Rambla property of John T. Gaffey, one of San Pedro's leading citizens.

Even after the passage of the River and Harbor Bill of 1896, yesterday's event was three years in the making. The entire project was stymied by the procedural and administrative stall tactics of longtime Huntington supporter, Secretary of War General Russell A. Alger. Only after outraged citizens of Los Angeles appealed directly to President McKinley was Alger commanded to commence the building of the breakwater.

When completed in 1910, the massive engineering feat will stretch 9,180 feet, starting from a point 1,900 feet offshore of the southwestern shore of the bay. Engineers close to the project say that the base of the breakwater will start at depths of 48 to 50 feet and be approximately 200 feet wide at its base. The breakwater will stand about 14 feet above the ocean at low tide and be 20 feet wide at its surface.

The huge rocks necessary for the construction will be quarried near Riverside, and in a supreme irony, will be carried to the bay on Southern Pacific railcars. Railroad officials say that it will be necessary to build trestles along the line of the breakwater to transport the rocks to their drop sites.

This first bargeload of rocks signals the start of breakwater construction.

Wilmington Staves off Suitors, Incorporates

San Pedro and Wilmington Now Los Angeles!

Local Resort Thrives

City Gets Control of Port

"New" L.A. River Flow Through Long Beac

New "Chicken of the Sea" Product— a Gamble?

Signal Hill Gusher Springs to Life

Women Right t

Prohibition Goes into Effect

Craig Launches General Hubbard

First Municipal Pier Dedicated

Balboa Studio Boasts Long Beach's Bigg Payroll

First Transc Flier Lands in

Huge Crowds Flock to Aviation Meet

of Los Angeles"

Webb Alien Land Bill nacted

iven ote

more Dead

tinental ng Beach

Chapter 3

Growth and Development

(1901-1925)

SAN PEDRO BAY		THE NATION	
1901	Willmore dead at 57 (p. 34)	1903	Wright brothers make world's first successful flight in motorized airplane
1903	New "Chicken of the Sea" product—a gamble? (p. 34)		
1905	Wilmington staves off suitors, incorporates (p. 34)	1907	Financial panic
1907	"Port of Los Angeles " created (p. 35)	1911	Mexican Revolution
1909	San Pedro and Wilmington now Los Angeles (p. 35)	1913	Webb Alien Land Bill enacted in California; excludes Japanese from land ownership
1910	Huge crowds flock to aviation meet (p. 36)		
1911	First transcontinental flier lands in Long Beach (p. 37)	1917	U.S. declares war on Germany
		1918	Influenza epidemic in U.S.
1911	Craig Launches *General Hubbard* (p. 37)	1920	Prohibition goes into effect
1911	First Municipal Pier dedicated (p. 38)	1920	Women given right to vote by 19th Amendment
1916	City gets control of Port (p. 39)	1921	Congress declares official end to war with Germany
1918	Balboa Studio boasts Long Beach's biggest payroll (p. 39)	1922	James Doolittle makes first one-day transcontinental flight
1921	Signal Hill gusher springs to life (p. 40)	1924	New immigration law takes effect; no Japanese allowed
1923	"New" L.A. River flows through Long Beach (p. 40)	1924	Congress declares native-born Indians citizens
1925	Local resort thrives (p. 41)		

Willmore Dead at 57

(1901, January 16) William E. Willmore, founder of the city of Long Beach, died today at the age of 57. Willmore passed away at the home of Mrs. Ida Crowe, who had taken in the former city planner and visionary after his quiet return to the city that he so loved.

Willmore is known for his valiant effort to develop a tract of land he called the "American Colony" into a city by the sea in the early 1880s. People soon began calling the new city "Willmore City."

Sales of the lots never reached the numbers that Willmore had envisioned, and he was forced to abandon his dream in May of 1884. Some believe that if Willmore had been able to sustain the effort a short while longer, his dream might have been realized.

After traveling to Arizona, Willmore suffered a debilitating sunstroke that permanently damaged his health. After returning to Southern California, he was found in a Downey poorhouse, where he had been committed by the County.

Prior to being housed by Mrs. Crowe, Willmore could be seen wandering the streets of the city that he founded ... without a home, without money, unable to work, and almost friendless. A proposed tax levy to help sustain the founder of the city was never acted upon.

Near death and still homeless, Willmore was on the verge of being returned to the poorhouse by the County when Mrs. Crowe's compassion rescued him.

A lifelong bachelor, Willmore died alone in the city that he started.

New "Chicken of the Sea" Product —A Gamble?

(1903) A new product is being distributed in local grocery stores by the Southern California Fish Company in the hope of reviving the fortunes of the firm's cannery business. The new fish product is canned albacore, a deep-sea fish related to the tuna family.

Recently the cannery has fallen on hard times as local sardine schools have disappeared. Having moved the company from the San Francisco Bay area several years ago and faced with declining catches and revenue, Alfred P. Halfhill (a co-owner of the company) began a search for another fish that could be canned.

Halfhill experimented with many species of fish, including halibut and cod, none of which turned out to be a viable fish for canning purposes. He then came across a tin of Italian "tunny," which did seem to possess a potential for a palatable canned-fish product. This tunny was, in fact, albacore.

Wilbur F. Wood, foreman of the cannery, began experiments with pre-cooking and steaming only the choice pieces from the albacore. After this process, the red flesh of the albacore remarkably turned white with a texture like that of chicken.

Seeing the potential for this "new" product, Halfhill named it "chicken of the sea." The company has canned 700 cases of the product and is distributing it throughout Southern California.

Because the public is still reluctant to accept this new canned fish, large portions of the initial consignments are regularly returned to the cannery.

Undaunted, Halfhill believes that the albacore will be accepted if only people taste it. To this end, he has persuaded grocers to give the fish away to customers with any purchase of coffee that they make. Halfhill is gambling that his "chicken of the sea" will someday be as common as a loaf of bread on American tables.

Wilmington Staves off Suitors, Incorporates

(1905, December) Wilmington is a city once again. Papers filed in the state capital have assured that the city will remain out of the boundaries of its neighbors, Long Beach and San Pedro.

Originally incorporated as a town in February 1872, Wilmington ran afoul of state laws when the city was cited for failure to hold elections for a new board of trustees. The city was disincorporated and reverted back to county administration.

Recently, both the cities of Long Beach and San Pedro have made attempts to annex Wilmington. However, those efforts have their roots in events going back several years.

As construction of the federal breakwater began in San Pedro, Long Beach leaders contemplated dredging a canal in the Cerritos Slough along Wilmington's shore. Such a waterway would give Long Beach access to international shipping by connecting the city to San Pedro.

In 1903 a proposal was made by a Long Beach citizen, William Galer, to annex Terminal Island. By so doing,

Long Beach would gain an already existing port facility, complete with rail lines and wharves.

An election this summer found Terminal Islanders favoring annexation by Long Beach . . . by one vote. San Pedro, armed with injunctions, protested vigorously, stating that East San Pedro had already petitioned San Pedro for annexation. The land fever had to focus elsewhere . . . to Wilmington.

Earlier this year Long Beach annexed a small portion of Wilmington that bordered on the harbor. Not content with this acquisition, city fathers proposed an even more audacious plan. Why not annex all of Wilmington?

Fearing for its independence and identity, leaders in Wilmington quickly drew up papers requesting reincorporation. The L.A. County Board of Supervisors approved the petition earlier this month at almost the same time that Long Beach voters elected to annex Wilmington. It now became a race to Sacramento for the formal filing of legal documents. Whichever city filed its papers first would win the battle for Wilmington.

Wilmington's representative, Senator and Judge Savage, knowing the importance of the timing issue, had the foresight to charter a special train from Tracy to Sacramento. He arrived at the California State Capitol at 5:30 in the morning to file Wilmington's reincorporation papers. At 10 a.m., Long Beach's representative arrived . . . via a regularly scheduled train.

"Port of Los Angeles" Created

(1907, December 10) The Los Angeles City Council yesterday took another large step in its effort to gain control of the harbor districts of San Pedro and Wilmington. The municipal body approved City Ordinance Number 19128, officially creating the Los Angeles Harbor Commission.

George H. Stewart, J.E. Carr, and F.W. Braun were named as the first commissioners to sit on the board. The stated mission of the new administrative body—the development of the harbor— is sure to assume the primary position on the new commission's agenda.

Yesterday's action is the second major maneuver that the City of Los Angeles has undertaken in the continuing debate over the eventual control and jurisdiction of the harbor.

Last year Los Angeles annexed a mile-wide, 16-mile-long strip of land that extends from the southern boundary of the city to the boundaries of San Pedro and Wilmington. Many observers close to the fight for consolidation of the harbors to Los Angeles viewed that action as the opening salvo in what has become a bitter campaign.

The extension of Los Angeles down this "shoestring" gives the city a continuous (and legal) link to the harbor district. It appears that the only obstacle standing in the way of consolidation is how the people will vote in the upcoming election.

San Pedro and Wilmington Now Los Angeles!

(1909, August 13) The cities of San Pedro and Wilmington will soon cease to be. By an overwhelming vote of 12,313 to 336, voters in San Pedro and Los Angeles decided yesterday that the future of the ports and harbor will be better served by the city fathers of Los Angeles.

Yesterday's vote culminates three years of political maneuvering with the control of the bustling port complex as the prize plum. The initial consolidation proposal was presented to San Pedro in early 1906. On May 6, the San Pedro Chamber of Commerce passed a resolution opposing the maneuver; however, on May 29, the Los Angeles Consolidation Committee applied more pressure by asking San Pedro to appoint a five-man consolidation committee to further study the proposal.

San Pedro, above, and Wilmington will soon become part of Los Angeles.

Although many die-hards in the harbor fumed at the idea of turning their ports over to Los Angeles, pragmatic business leaders early on realized that the huge sums of money needed to improve the harbor could only be had if control of the ports was turned over to the larger city.

And to bolster the earnestness of their request, in 1906 the City of Los Angeles annexed a section of land just north of the harbor. It was soon called Harbor City. This tract of land has the distinct configuration that includes a narrow strip of land that touches the harbor at a point just east of the West Basin Channel.

During the campaign for consolidation, Los Angeles made it clear that plans were being formulated to build a deep-water canal from the harbor to Harbor City. Such a canal would allow oceangoing vessels to travel up to what would soon be a brand new international port.

For its part, the City of Los Angeles has promised to provide San Pedro and Wilmington with a number of important and valuable benefits. These include the commitment of $10 million over the next 10 years for harbor improvements by dredging and landfilling and the construction of new facilities. The 1,900-foot gap between the start of the federal breakwater and the shoreline will also be closed by the construction of a new, connecting breakwater. A city-owned and administered fishermen's wharf and fish market will also be built by the city. Further, a new ferry service between San Pedro and Terminal Island will operate (with a guarantee that the fare will not exceed two cents). A new police station will be erected in the area to serve both communities, and new libraries will be built throughout San Pedro. New fire stations will likewise be constructed in both San Pedro and Wilmington. A system of public schools (K-12) will be provided for the students of the harbor area, with equipment, facilities, and teacher salaries equal to those throughout the city. Finally, Los Angeles has promised to establish offices of the Parks Department, City Engineer, and Health Department in the San Pedro district.

The official day of consolidation will be August 28, thus marking the beginning of a new era for the former cities of San Pedro and Wilmington.

Huge Crowds Flock to Aviation Meet

(1910, January 21) An estimated 175,000 people converged on a high plateau of Rancho San Pedro over an 11-day period to witness America's first aviation meet.

The Dominguez Hills site of the gathering gave Angelenos their first opportunity to see what the air age might hold for them. A total of 11 aeroplanes, 10 pilots, 3 dirigibles, and 7 balloons took part in the festivities.

Sponsored by the Los Angeles Merchants and Manufacturers Association, the meet was the brainchild of two exhibition pilots, Roy Knabenshue and Charles Willard. The aviators said that they had no prospects for the winter season and hatched the idea of a show in sunny Southern California in midwinter.

Surely a highlight of the show was the presence of Louis Paulhan of France. Already an established celebrity on the Continent due to his showing at the Rheims, France, air meet last year, Paulhan was the top prizewinner here with more than $14,000 in winnings.

Not to be outdone by his Gallic counterpart, American Glenn H. Curtiss of Hammondsport, New York, had the honor of being the first aviator to fly at the meet. By the end of the show, Curtiss had amassed prize monies of $6,000.

Crowds of 20,000 attended the meet every day. Pacific Electric's Red Cars could be seen discharging full loads of spectators all throughout the 11 days of the event.

The meet was truly an exciting, historical event for the people of Los Angeles. One of the pilots even flew his craft over the Pacific Ocean in a

Aeroplanes, dirigibles, and balloons thrill thousands at Dominguez Hills in the nation's first air meet.

daring display of courage. Another took his aeroplane to 4,600 feet above sea level. And, yet another exhibitor flew his machine at a spectacular 70 miles per hour.

So popular and exciting was the air meet that the promoters and sponsors are even now contemplating another aviation exhibition as soon as December of this year.

First Transcontinental Flier Lands in Long Beach

Calbraith Perry "Cal" Rodgers

(1911, December 12) The country's first coast-to-coast aeroplane flight was completed yesterday when Calbraith Perry Rodgers landed his *Vin Fizz Flyer* on the shores of Long Beach.

The total duration of the transcontinental journey took 84 days. Rodgers, a pupil of the Wright brothers, left Sheepshead Bay, New York, on September 9 and arrived in Pasadena on November 5. Many newspapers and followers of the flight considered the journey to be completed on that day. However, Rodgers insisted on touching down on the Pacific shoreline to officially finish the flight.

Rodgers' endeavor was inspired by the $50,000 prize that William Randolph Hearst offered for anyone making the shore-to-shore air journey within 30 days. Although Rodgers will not collect the prize money, he nevertheless has the distinction of being the first person to complete the transcontinental flight.

Rodgers' triumph was far from smooth. The 4,321-mile course saw him crash 18 times, the most serious incident occurring in Compton on the last leg of the journey. That mishap laid Rodgers up for a month before he was able to make the final flight. It was during his recuperation that Rodgers selected Long Beach as the site for his final landing.

Even as Rodgers landed in Chicago on the 28th day, he vowed to complete the flight, prize money or not. With a support group following him with spare parts, mechanics, family, and friends, Rodgers was determined to claim the honor of being the first to fly coast to coast.

Rodgers' aeroplane, specially designed by the Wright brothers, was named the *Vin Fizz Flyer* because Rodgers had convinced the Armour Company to sponsor the flight. Armour, the manufacturer of the soft drink Vin Fizz, saw the feat as a way to boost sales of its product.

The *General Hubbard* hit the water with a mighty splash at Craig Shipbuilding's Long Beach drydocks.

Craig Launches *General Hubbard*

(1911) Craig Shipbuilding of Long Beach has launched the *General Hubbard* from its drydocks in Long Beach Harbor. The new vessel is the first completely steel-hulled steamship to be built south of San Francisco. The 256-foot-long ship will also have the distinction of being the first vessel to sail through the newly dredged channel from Long Beach's inner harbor to the open ocean.

The launching of the *General Hubbard* marks a significant point in the development of the fledgling har-

bor. The Craig shipyard is the first large-scale company to locate its operations in the harbor, and, more importantly, is the first major industry in the city.

The *General Hubbard* is also a personal triumph for the company's founder and owner, John F. Craig. It was only a few years ago that Craig first visited Long Beach to improve his ailing health. A native of Toledo, Ohio, Craig already had a successful shipbuilding operation in that city. The Craig company had launched more than 100 Great Lakes vessels in addition to 17 oceangoing ships that sailed around Cape Horn for service in the intercoastal Pacific trade.

However, the ideal climate and the potential for business expansion in Long Beach made a deep impression on Craig. When the need to expand the company arose, Craig remembered the city on the West Coast.

In true pioneering style, the shipbuilder closed the company in Ohio and began to relocate his operation to Southern California. Chartering a train in Toledo, Craig moved his entire company to Long Beach. Twenty-six foremen and their families as well as essential machinery made the move at a personal cost to Craig of $250,000.

The site for the company was a matter of shrewd negotiations between Craig, two other cities, and Long Beach. Both San Diego and San Pedro entered the bidding to entice Craig to locate his company in their cities. Long Beach finally won out after posting a bid of $100,000 and an offer of 43 acres of land, including 2,000 feet of waterside frontage.

Significantly, the first vessel to be built and launched by the shipyard was a dredger for the Western Marine Company. It is this very dredger that is now being used for deepening the port's channels and improving the inner harbor.

Of possibly greater significance to the city was the fact that the first major industry to locate in Long Beach was a shipyard in the harbor. When Craig started his operation there in 1907, the only access from Long Beach harbor to the ocean was through the Cerritos Slough, past Wilmington and San Pedro and, thence, to the open sea.

With a shipyard now in Long Beach, pressure was exerted to build a bridge across the Salt Lake Railroad line running between the city and Terminal Island. The presence of the rail line was the major impediment blocking direct ocean access from Long Beach.

The War Department finally interceded and asked the Salt Lake Railroad to build a bridge across the channel. Three years ago, the 187-foot bascule bridge was erected by the railroad, thus opening Long Beach to ocean commerce.

First Municipal Pier Dedicated

(1911, June 24) As thousands of citizens and curious onlookers watched, city officials today formally dedicated the city's first municipal pier in Long Beach harbor.

The crowd of well-wishers began assembling at the foot of Pine Avenue at 1:00 p.m. in anticipation of the parade that would lead them to the site of the dedication ceremony. A large contingent of automobiles was also a part of the parade. The entire group was accompanied to the harbor by the Long Beach Municipal Band.

Although the 500-foot-long dock was formally dedicated today, several vessels have already called at the new pier. The S.S. *Iaqua,* a lumber schooner, has the distinction of being the first ship to use the facility. She discharged her cargo of 280,000 board feet of redwood on June 2. Yesterday the steamer *Santa Barbara* tied up at the pier and began discharging lumber consigned to the Long Beach

The lumber schooner S.S. *Iaqua* has become the first ship to use the new municipal pier.

Improvement Company.

The development of the harbor was given impetus by the issuance of $245,000 of municipal bonds in 1909, $200,000 of which are earmarked for the purchase of 2,200 feet of harbor frontage. There has even been talk of the city buying all of the property in the harbor in order to dictate the direction of the port's development.

At today's ceremony, Mayor Windham and other city notables emphasized the day's importance to the city by saying that the practical use of the harbor was necessary to ensure the future growth and prosperity of the city.

City Gets Control of Port

(1916) The City of Long Beach today gained control of all of the harbor as part of the Los Angeles Dock and Terminal Company's bankruptcy proceedings.

The severe winter storms of 1914 and similar storms earlier this year were the final blows that finally forced the company to petition for bankruptcy. Damage to waterfront facilities and subsequent flooding and siltation of them proved to be too formidable for the ambitious, yet struggling, company.

The Dock and Terminal Company began its operations in the port in 1905 when it purchased 800 acres of marshland west of the city at the mouth of the Los Angeles River. Initial plans called for the creation of a 1,400-foot turning basin in the inner harbor, dredging of the Los Angeles River to a depth of 30 feet and a width of 300 feet, dredging of the Cerritos Slough, which connected Long Beach to San Pedro and Wilmington, and the construction of three ship channels and warehouse facilities.

Actual dredging began in 1906, but the company was beset continuously by the silt that flowed down the river. The Dock and Terminal Company simply could not gain the upper hand over the winter floods that brought silt and debris to areas that had been recently dredged.

As early as 1909, city leaders had discussed the idea of the City purchasing all of the lands in the harbor. If this was accomplished, then the City, and not private landowners, such as the railroads, would be able to direct the development of the port.

The bankruptcy petition states that Long Beach will receive title to all of the channels built by the Dock and Terminal Company as well as a five-acre parcel of land near slip number 5. All dredging rights and responsibilities in the harbor will also revert back to the City.

Balboa Studio Boasts Long Beach's Biggest Payroll

(1918) Balboa Films of Long Beach now boasts the city's largest payroll, employing 250 regular employees and daily wages totaling $2,000. The local independent film production company is located on the corners of Alamitos Boulevard and Sixth Street and is a leader in providing one-reelers and serials to other studios and distributing firms.

The studio was started in 1913 by H.M. Horkheimer, a former theater producer from New York, with an investment of $7,000. Elwood Horkheimer, brother of the founder, soon moved to Long Beach to help with the company.

The studio was not the city's first. Earlier, the Edison Company set up shop on the corner of Alamitos and Sixth. Heading up that studio was J. Searle Dawley, who remained in the city long enough to turn the site over to Horkheimer in 1913.

In the short span of four years, the two enterprising brothers built the Balboa Amusements Producing Company into Southern California's largest movie studio. Horkheimer is known for shooting his films in and around the Long Beach area. Favorite locations are the Pike, the Naples canals, and, of course, the beaches. Westerns are generally shot near Signal Hill on wide-open tracts of land.

As an independent studio, Balboa receives many requests from other studios to produce films for them.

Many of these are then distributed by companies such as Fox, Paramount, Mutual, Comedy-Art, World, and General Films.

Some of motion pictures' biggest stars are regular performers in Balboa's films. Roscoe "Fatty" Arbuckle, Theda Bara, Mabel Normand, Slim Pickett, Jackie Saunders, and Ruth Roland are some of the stars of the studio. Arbuckle and Bara live across the street from each other on the eastern end of Ocean Boulevard and are occasionally seen on the city's streets.

The Horkheimers soon outgrew the original Edison building, and subsequent expansions soon found them occupying all four corners of Alamitos

Balboa Films of Long Beach is located on the corners of Alamitos Boulevard and Sixth Street.

and Sixth. So successful is the operation that the studio is today known as the "House of Serials" throughout the industry.

Currently the company has 100,000 props indexed and 8 stages on which to produce their films. A total of 18 buildings now comprise the Balboa complex, and the total worth of the company is estimated to be $500,000.

SIGNAL HILL GUSHER SPRINGS TO LIFE

Last night Shell Oil's Alamitos No. 1 spewed "black gold" into the skies above Signal Hill.

(1921, June 24) The skies above Signal Hill rumbled and roared last night with the sound of newly discovered wealth. Shell Oil's exploratory well, Alamitos No. 1, dramatically sprang to life, blasting crude oil, "black gold," nearly 100 feet into the night air. Jubilant oil field workers said that the drill hit the oil at a depth of 2,745 feet. Alamitos No. 1 is located on the corner of Temple and Hill streets.

The well is still uncapped, and it will be several days before oil workers can control the black goo from falling over the homes and buildings surrounding the well. However, the sticky mess will bring smiles to the faces of landowners on the hill as land values are sure to skyrocket because of the discovery. Already there is talk that the entire hill is sitting on an ocean of oil.

There has long been speculation that oil was to be found beneath the city. An early well was sunk in 1898 at Broadway and Grand avenues, but was abandoned at the 1,500-foot depth because of lack of suitable equipment to go any deeper.

In 1906 traces of oil were found in a water well that was being dug near Seventh Street and Park Avenue. More recently three exploratory wells were sunk by Union Oil on property leased from the Bixby Estate. All three turned up dry.

With heady talk of overnight fortunes to be made already on the lips of speculators, the one sure beneficiary of all of this will be the City of Long Beach, which owns 140 acres near Alamitos No. 1.

"New" L.A. River Flows Through Long Beach

(1923) The Los Angeles River, long the culprit in the battle to develop Long Beach harbor, has been tamed. The river, previously running unchecked into the inner harbor, now runs to the sea through the west side of Long Beach.

The "new" river is actually a flood control project of the Los Angeles County Flood Control District. The government agency, created in 1917, attempts to find solutions to the unpredictable winter floods that plague the Southland.

The Port of Long Beach has been a perennial victim of the whims of the river's flooding. Constant dredging has been required to keep the inner channels free of the silt and debris that flowed down the river every winter.

The Flood Control District's bold plan called for the river to be diverted around the east end of the harbor and away from the harbor's channels. Once this had been done, the now channeled river could flow straight into the ocean. To accomplish this engineering feat, a $4.5-million county bond issue was approved by voters to finance the project.

City and harbor officials in both Los Angeles and Long Beach now believe that the development of the harbor can proceed in an efficient and orderly manner. Not having to be concerned about the maintenance of channel depths will allow more funds to be used for dredging the inner harbor to accommodate deeper-draft vessels.

Local Resort Thrives

(1925) The White Point Hot Springs and Health Resort continues to thrive as people from Los Angeles and Orange counties come to enjoy its sulphur pools along the Palos Verdes shoreline.

Built in 1917 as a joint project between Tamiji Tagami and Ramon Sepulveda, owner of the property, the resort provides pools of sulphurous waters that are touted to relieve stomach disorders, kidney troubles, rheumatism, arthritis, paralysis, spinal nerve irritation, gonorrhea, intestinal problems, and even nervous disorders.

Tagami and Sepulveda pipe the waters directly from the springs into their resorts' pools. Families are encouraged to stay at the 40-room hotel on the site or at several cottages along the shore. Their children can play in the wading pool built especially for them. A fishing pier and boat landing affords patrons other activities during their stay.

White Point's sulphur springs were noticed immediately by the Japanese abalone fishermen who worked the area in the early 1900s. They so prized the natural spring waters that on occasion they even carried it back to their homes for nightly baths. The fishing community thrived for many years, but by 1915 it had all but ceased to exist.

The grounds were severely overfished by then, and anti-Japanese sentiments resulted in legislation banning abalone fishing. But the former residents never forgot the wonderful sulphur springs to be found there.

It was then that Tagami approached Sepulveda and proposed the plan to capitalize on White Point's natural attractions. The huge crowds attest to the wisdom of the duo's joint project.

The White Point Hot Springs and Health Resort draws visitors from Los Angeles and Orange counties.

Aviation Pioneer Crashes to His Death

Longshoreman Killed in Strike Melee

Japanese to be Removed from Terminal Island

New Longsho Union Formed

Pt. Goes

"Rosie the Rivete Sends Planes Off to War

Pedro Shipyards Humming

KILLER QUAKE HITS LONG BEACH

"Townse Followers to 750,000

Deadman's Island Demolished

Pacific Southwest Exposition Opens

Feds Open New Jail

Japanese Fishing Communi Thrives

Navy Shipyard to be Built

LONG BEACH FLEET HEADQ

Triumph and Tragedy

(1928-1945)

Pacific Southwest Exposition Opens

(1928, July 28) With the blaring of horns, whistles, and sirens throughout the city, Governor C.C. Young officially opened the Pacific Southwest Exposition at 12 noon yesterday.

Thousands of first-day visitors cheered as the governor welcomed them to the festival he called a "world's fair."

The spectacular event is sponsored by the Long Beach Chamber of Commerce and supported by several local civic leaders. Six hundred fifty thousand dollars was raised to create a mock Moslem city on 63 acres at the end of Seventh Street in the port's inner harbor. Designed by architect Hugh R. Davies, the stucco on plasterboard make-believe Mecca was built in only 10 1/2 weeks.

The show is designed to spotlight the tremendous growth and contributions that the American Southwest has made in the past several years. In addition, 26 nations have spent $15 million to showcase their achievements and products in the individual national pavilions.

By yesterday's opening, Norway, Sweden, France, Switzerland, Denmark, Holland, Ecuador, Belgium, Latvia, Italy, China, the Philippines, New Zealand, and Guatemala had exhibits for people to visit. And, as he will throughout the exposition, Kamel Ahmedd gave the Islamic call to prayer twice throughout the day from a replica of a mosque tower.

Last night actress Gloria Swanson threw a switch that illuminated the entire central quadrangle and reflecting pool area.

Other attractions for those attending the festival will be concerts by the Long Beach Municipal Band, a free Wild West Show, a U.S. Forest Service exhibit of natural habitats, several North African "bazaars," and a young lady diving into a pool of water with her bathing suit ablaze.

The show not only celebrates the past accomplishments of the country, but also points to the vibrancy and economic strength that America will take with her into the next decade.

The exposition will run until September and is open every day.

Left: The Pacific Southwest Exposition covers 63 acres at the end of Long Beach's Seventh Street. Opposite: Visitors to the Exposition can be entertained by Oriental and Hawaiian dancers and musicians for 10 cents.

Aviation Pioneer Crashes to His Death

(1928, December 8) Earl S. Daugherty, Long Beach aviation pioneer and the man most responsible for the Long Beach Municipal Airport, crashed to his death early this morning. Two passengers were also on board the plane during the stunt flight over North Long Beach.

Eyewitnesses said that as Daugherty's plane entered a barrel roll, the left wing collapsed, sending the plane crashing to earth.

Daugherty was smitten by the aviation bug after attending the Dominguez Air Meet in 1910. Together with Frank Champion, Daugherty began to build airplanes in the basement of an apartment owned by Earl's father.

During World War I, Daugherty was commissioned as a lieutenant in the Army Signal Crops, which was responsible for the development of military aircraft. He also trained pilots at Rockwell Field in San Diego and March Field in Riverside.

Following the war Daugherty opened the city's first air field in North Long Beach at the corner of American Avenue and Bixby Road, naming it Chateau Thierry. Several years later Daugherty and his father bought a larger piece of land at Willow and American and named it Daugherty Field, giving rides and flying lessons

to the public.

When Long Beach formed its first Airport Commission, Daugherty was a logical choice for a seat. He served together with Al Ebrite and J.J. Montijo on the inaugural board.

In 1924 the city wanted to expand and improve Daugherty Field. Citing the fact that he had already expended $50,000 of his own on the field, Daugherty convinced the city to locate a new municipal airport on 80 acres belonging to the Water Department northeast of Signal Hill near Spring and Cherry avenues. The result was Southern California's first municipal airport.

At his death, Daugherty was 42 years old. Also on board the aircraft were *Press-Telegram* editor, Warren Montfort, and Elmer Starr, part owner and manager of the Pacific Engraving Company, both of whom insisted on flying this morning.

When fellow aviators heard of the news, some were overheard saying that Daugherty had always claimed that he would go out on a spectacular final dive.

Long Beach aviation pioneer Earl S. Daugherty has died in an early morning plane crash.

46

Deadman's Island Demolished

(1929) After two years of constant boring and blasting, the demolition of Deadman's Island was finally completed. The rock and debris from the island is deposited on the southwestern end of Terminal Island and now forms 62 acres of new land called Reservation Point.

A longtime landmark of San Pedro harbor, the island was noted in the logs of the early Spanish explorers to the bay. As Los Angeles' commerce grew more and more vibrant, the amount of shipping traffic into the port grew in proportion.

By 1908 harbor improvement projects had widened the main channel to 500 feet. However, the entrance to the harbor, anchored at the eastern end by Deadman's Island, was still at 400 feet.

Not only was the island creating a bottleneck as ships tried to enter and leave the port, but it also increasingly became a hazard to navigation.

The ownership of the island was turned over to the federal government in 1916, and a year later gun emplacements were constructed there as the United States entered the war in Europe. It was at this time that the Harbor Commission voted to widen the channel to a minimum width of 1,200 feet. The days of Deadman's Island were numbered.

True to its name, Deadman's Island yielded 23 bodies when excavation began in 1927. These bodies included those of 6 U.S. Marines killed in the Battle of Dominguez of 1846; 2 Spaniards in conquistador boots buried with an ancient sword; a woman with golden hair; an English sea captain, "Black Hawk," believed to be the last resident of San Nicolas Island; and 11 other people. All of the remains were duly reinterred.

Japanese Fishing Community Thrives

(1931) Based on interviews with Japanese fishermen on Terminal Island, the first residents were from fishing villages in their homeland of Japan. Having fished in the White Point area since the turn of the century, the Japanese immigrants then moved into East San Pedro in 1906 and started what is today a thriving commercial and social community.

Bringing their skills and traditions honed over years of fishing in southern Japan, these pioneers found the waters off San Pedro to be ideal fishing grounds. Like most immigrants before them, many had left poverty and lack of opportunity behind in order to make new lives for themselves in America.

The first residents drove pilings into the shores of Terminal Island across from San Pedro and built 20 homes for the fishermen working in the area. One year later, approximately 600 Japanese fishermen called East San Pedro home.

The successful and lucrative fishing industry in San Pedro was a boon to all who lived in the area. By the 1920s, the Japanese, Yugoslavs, Italians, and Portuguese had created one of the most successful fishing communities on the entire West Coast. The

These Japanese women are making fish cakes from barracuda in a Terminal Island cannery.

Japanese population now stood at 3,000 in East San Pedro.

This year nearly 40 percent of the 1,582 fishing licenses issued were to Japanese immigrants. Their American-born offspring who also hold licenses are counted among the 459 Americans issued permits.

Today's Terminal Island Japanese community is one of independence and self-sufficiency. Markets, stores, restaurants, doctors, and dentists serve the needs of the residents. Social, community, and business organizations such as the Japanese Association, PTA, and the Japanese Fishermen's Association thrive among the residents.

But the community is certainly not an island unto itself. Along with the Buddhist temple, a growing Baptist church also serves the residents; and thus, western holidays are celebrated along with traditional Japanese festivals and holidays. The elementary school on the island is 98 percent Japanese, but high school students make the daily ferry trip to attend Dana Junior High and San Pedro High. Most of the students also attend one of two Japanese language schools after their regular school day ends.

So, together with learning the traditional martial arts of Japan, the island's boys also participate in baseball leagues. And the latest dance craze is practiced as much, or even more, than the traditional dances of Japan.

Such is the Japanese community on Terminal Island, a commmunity that is rooted in the traditions of its homeland, though basically an American community on the move.

EXTRA!

Killer Quake Hits Long Beach

(1933, March 11) An earthquake of massive proportions hit Long Beach last night, spewing death and destruction in its wake.

Just as most people were preparing for the evening's meal, the quake hit at 5:55 p.m. When the 11 seconds of terror stopped and the dust had cleared, an estimated 50 Long Beach residents were dead and hundreds more injured.

Most of the victims were killed by falling debris as buildings crumbled throughout the city and streets twisted

Earthquake damage in downtown Long Beach was devastating.

and buckled. Initial surveys indicate that up to 3,500 people are without homes in the city.

The quake was reportedly felt throughout the state. In Los Angeles and Orange counties, the death toll is expected to reach 100. Statewide, thousands of homes were destroyed and thousands more damaged. Damage was reported in 25 cities. Hundreds of commercial and public buildings were completely destroyed, and thousands damaged, some beyond repair.

Mercifully, the quake hit at a time when the city's schools were not in session, as the most severe damage was sustained by school buildings throughout Long Beach.

Terrified residents spent the evening in their backyards or outdoors rather than reenter damaged buildings. Aftershocks continued to shake the city and will probably do so for months to come say many experts.

Aid and assistance was swift in coming. Immediately after the shock, Admiral R.H. Leigh of the U.S. Pacific Fleet, anchored in the harbor, offered medical supplies, tents, and food rushed to wherever they were needed.

The Salvation Army, Red Cross, National Guard, American Legion, and personnel from Fort MacArthur also joined in the relief effort. Temporary shelters and field kitchens are now in operation at parks in the city.

Preliminary estimates of the earthquake's damage are put at $7 million to $8 million. However, others say that the final tally may run as high as $40 million to $45 million.

Longshoreman Killed in Strike Melee

(1934, May 15) A violent eruption yesterday between striking International Longshoremen's Association (ILA) members and 400 strikebreakers resulted in one striker being shot to death.

Richard "Dickie" Parker, 20, had just joined the ILA Local 38-82 one day before being gunned down near the strikebreakers' lodging facilities at Berth 140.

San Pedro's waterfront strike is part of a larger coastwide work stoppage action coordinated by the leader of the San Francisco ILA local, Harry Bridges. The transplanted Australian longshoreman called for the strike to demand better working conditions and pay increases for his fellow workers.

Commencing on May 9, the strike is particularly aimed at eliminating what is referred to by the ILA as the "Fink Hall," or employer-controlled hiring hall, and the "Speed-Up" and "Shape-Up."

The "Speed-Up" is the practice of pushing longshore gangs to work faster and faster, often at the risk of injury. Gangs are forced to compete against each other during a "Speed-Up."

The "Shape-Up" is one of the most-hated institutions among the longshoremen. Every morning men hoping to obtain work gather at the hiring hall for job calls. The job foremen selectively distribute the available jobs to the waiting men. The longshoremen have repeatedly accused the foremen of regularly requesting bribes or other favors in exchange for jobs. Referred to as a slave market by its critics, the practice was abandoned by the Port of London in 1891 as being "uncivilized."

In San Pedro and elsewhere up the West Coast, the ILA has been dormant since 1919, when an attempted strike action failed because of lack of support from the Seafarers' Union and the Teamsters' Union. However, with the passage of President Roosevelt's National Industrial Recovery Act in January of this year, unions are given the right to organize and bargain collectively with their employers, free from interference, restraint, or coercion.

Eyewitnesses report that 300 strikers were armed with baseball bats and clubs. As they approached the encampment of the strikebreakers, private security guards opened up with gunfire. Soon after police stationed at the site began firing tear gas projectiles into the crowd. Rocks, stones, pieces

Before the ILA strike turned deadly, San Francisco ILA local leader Harry Bridges led picketing union members in this show of solidarity.

of wood, and anything else that could pass as weapons were being used by both groups.

After the tear gas had cleared and order was restored to the area, it was reported that 8 people had been wounded by bullets, and 23 others were injured by other means. One of the gunshot victims, ILA member John Knudsen, 51, is listed in critical condition.

New Longshore Union Formed

(1934, June) As the coastwide maritime strike nears two months in duration, a dramatic change has been effected by striking longshoremen. The International Longshoremen's Association (ILA) has been ousted as the representative union of all West Coast longshoremen. A newly formed group, the International Longshoremen's and Warehousemen's Union (ILWU), led by controversial labor organizer Harry Bridges, will now represent longshoremen working at all West Coast ports.

The New York-based ILA has traditionally represented dock workers across the nation, but the bitter and violent strike by West Coast longshoremen sharply focused the rank-and-file criticism of the East Coast leadership.

In San Pedro the deaths of two longshoremen in a May 14 clash with strikebreakers galvanized the demands of workers up and down the coast.

At a special meeting in February of the West Coast District of the ILA called by Bridges, five militant objectives were set forth by the members: recognition of the union by the employers, union-controlled hiring halls, a raise in pay from 85 cents an hour to one dollar, a 30-hour work week, and a coastwide contract covering all ports and expiring on the same date.

Further, the members resolved that no agreement worked out between the ILA leaders and employers could be valid unless endorsed by the rank and file.

From the outset, it appeared that a major rift was in the making between the established ILA leadership and Bridges' own style of radical confrontation. William J. Lewis, the ILA district president, was increasingly criticized for his conservative stance in negotiating with employers. Further, the members were becoming more and more frustrated with the ILA policy of entering into binding agreements without polling the members.

As the strike gains more momentum, the power and influence of the ILA correspondingly seems to ebb.

When Mayor Angelo Rossi invited ILA President Joseph C. Ryan to San Francisco to assist in settling the strike, the proposed "peace plan" formulated by Ryan was soundly rejected by the members.

On June 16, Ryan announced that a "binding" agreement had been signed with the Water Employers' Union. Again the ILA plan was unanimously turned down by the rank and file. The following day Ryan was booed off the stage in San Francisco for "selling out" the union.

Currently, most of the maritime unions have joined the longshoremen on strike. Sailors, cooks and stewards, radio operators, masters, mates and pilots, and the Marine Workers' Industrial Union are all involved in some form of work action.

Hundreds of ships are sitting idle at ports along the coast with their entire cargos untouched. The Teamsters have agreed not to move any cargos that are off-loaded by strikebreakers.

As more and more waterfront workers walk off their jobs, there are increasing discussions about expanding the strike to embrace unions throughout the city. Already it is rumored that Bridges and some other labor leaders are planning a major general strike to shut down San Francisco.

Concern over the fact that many of the strike's leaders are members of the Communist party, most notably Bridges, is adding additional tension to an already strained situation. Accusations and "red-baiting" are daily occurrences in the city.

Ironically, even the established leadership of the American Federation of Labor (AFL) has aligned itself with city bureaucrats and employers in calling the strikers Bolsheviks. And Joseph Ryan, the national ILA president, has been recently quoted as saying that the strike is nothing but a Communist plot.

Feds Open New Jail

(1938, June 1) The "grand" opening wasn't as grand as some others experienced in the past. No music, festive airs, or spirited laughter. But, it was an opening nevertheless. And so, as 50 federal prisoners marched through the gates of the new federal jail on Reservation Point, the prison was officially opened.

The 28-acre facility is classified by the Federal Bureau of Prisons as "medium security." The land was acquired from the Los Angeles Harbor Department when the Bureau sought to locate a site for a new jail in the Southern California region. Eventually the jail will house 600 male inmates and 24 female prisoners.

The land on which the new prison sits was once the famous San Pedro landmark, Deadman's Island. So named because U.S. servicemen killed in the Battle of Dominguez of the U.S.-Mexico War were buried on the island, the tiny landfall was a longtime fixture in the San Pedro harbor. Every ship that ever docked in the port passed by the island on its way to the inner harbor. A jetty was eventually built from Terminal Island to Deadman's Island, forming what would eventually become today's main channel.

However, when deepening and widening the channel was proposed, it became apparent that Deadman's Island would have to be removed. The blasting and leveling of the island began in 1927, with the spoils and dredge material being deposited on the southern end of Terminal Island. Eventually this landfill formed a 62-acre rectangle and was named Reservation Point when it was completed in 1930.

"Townsend Plan" Followers Swell To 750,000

(1939) Advocates of the so-called Townsend Plan recently revealed that their latest membership polls show that three-quarters of a million persons have paid their 25 cents to join and support one of the Townsend Clubs throughout the nation. The clubs and their members support a controversial social service proposal that provides for the well-being of the old and poor of our country.

The brain-child of retired Long Beach physician Francis Townsend, the plan is formally known as the Old Age Revolving Pension (OARP).

In essence the plan calls for an across-the-board $200 federal monthly payment to all Americans 60 years and older. The only stipulation is that the recipients spend all of the stipend with-

in 30 days in the United States.

By so doing, Townsend believes that $2 billion to $3 billion of "fresh money" will be pumped into the economy every month. Further, with every dollar being respent 10 times, the plan will benefit the nation in the sum of $20 billion monthly. Additionally, this circulation of money stimulates the economy by creating 20 million new jobs throughout the country.

Townsend began his crusade in 1934, when, as a 66-year-old civil servant, his job was suddenly eliminated by the city council. With only $100 to his name, and chances for future employment severely limited, Townsend became acutely aware of the plight of the elderly poor.

With a motto of "Youth for Work, Age for Leisure," the OARP found fertile grounds in the population of Long Beach for his radical plan. Soon Townsend was spreading his word with a missionary zeal. He exhorted his fellow elderly to realize the power of their votes by telling them, "We elderly might be too old to work, but we're not too old to vote."

Soon the early ripples grew to waves of support for the plan. Six million signatures were gathered in support of the program. A national newspaper with a circulation of 500,000 now spreads the word to even more people, and Townsend Clubs now number 12,000 throughout the entire nation, including 25 in Long Beach alone.

Critics of Townsend have called him an economic illiterate, a crackpot, a charlatan, quack, and demagogue. A

congressional committee recently reported that should the OARP plan be put into operation, one-half of the nation's income would be going to 10 percent of the population.

Nevertheless, Dr. Townsend and his followers continue to rally the old and poor of America. The latest estimates of those who support the plan is put at 15 to 25 million people.

Navy Shipyard to be Built

(1940) Following the recommendations of Navy officials, Congress has appropriated funds to construct a new naval shipyard in Long Beach. Navy officials emphasize that the new repair facility will be crucial to our nation's western defense system.

The new yard will be the Navy's only one in Southern California. It will service ships in the area formed by the triangle of the Panama Canal to a point 3,000 miles due west and then back to Long Beach. Contributing to the needs of America's defense, the City of Long Beach made the 108 acres of land available to the Navy Department for one dollar.

The highlight of the yard will be a massive dry dock capable of servicing several vessels at the same time. The length of the facility will be 1,105 feet with a width of 155 feet. Two and one-half hours will be required to fill the dry dock with 50.59 million gallons of water, and it will take four hours to pump all of the water out of it.

The Navy selected Long Beach for several reasons, one of the most compelling being the favorable climate of the area. The average mean temperature is 62.5 degrees with limited rainfall. This means that the work of the shipyard will not be unduly hampered by bad weather.

Naval officers also cited the readily available fuel, water, and power supplies that will be needed to operate the yard. The strong labor pool was also cited as a plus for the site.

In order to make the facility safer for the naval ships that will be worked on, a 6,000-foot extension of the federal breakwater will be built. A submarine net will also be strung across the entrance to the shipyard. Of course, these measures will also benefit the many Navy ships that are anchored in the harbor.

The Navy is set to start construction in August of this year, with the yard becoming operational in February of 1943.

Long Beach Selected Fleet Headquarters

(1941, September 25) The Navy Department made it official today, but in the minds of many, it was inevitable. Long Beach is now the headquarters for the Navy's Pacific Fleet. Navy Department General Order No. 154 officially establishes a naval operating base in Long Beach.

Culminating a tug-of-war with San Pedro and other West Coast ports, today's action was hardly a surprise to old Navy hands and Long Beach boosters. Long Beach has been identified with the Navy ever since the Great White Fleet of Teddy Roosevelt anchored off of Southern California in 1908. Although San Pedro, Redondo Beach, and Venice Beach, like Long Beach, hosted four battleships apiece, it was the latter that was the site for a formal reception for Fleet Admiral Robley B. Evans, a former hero in the Spanish-American War. From this point forward, the Navy and Long Beach began to cement the relationship that led to today's General Order.

In 1919 President Woodrow Wilson deployed a contingent of nine battlewagons together with support vessels to San Pedro Bay to establish a permanent operating base. Two years later, Admiral W.E. Eberle, commander of the base, moved his headquarters onshore, setting up offices in Long Beach's exclusive Virginia Hotel. City fathers rose to the occasion by hailing the city as "Home Port of the Battle Fleet."

Even before this time, Long Beach was already the forerunner in the race for the Pacific Fleet. Senior naval officers saw San Francisco and San Diego harbors as not being deep enough, Seattle as being plagued with inclement weather, and San Pedro as being overly concerned with commercial shipping activities.

In 1932, 50 Navy vessels were home-anchored in Long Beach, and 900 Navy families called Long Beach their home (the most in any city in the country). By now Long Beach had certainly deserved the name, "Navy Capital of the United States."

However, in the 1930s, Los Angeles Harbor Department officials reluctantly granted a 30-year lease to the Navy for an airfield on Terminal Island. Today this is Reeves Field, the air base for the Pacific Fleet.

Not to be outdone, Long Beach Harbor built, at its own expense, an $80,000 landing for the Navy, where sailors could be shuttled between their vessels and the shore. Nearby it also built a $15,000 athletic field for naval personnel.

If the Navy Department needed any more convincing about where to locate its fleet headquarters, it came last year. It was in August that the Navy took possession of 108 acres of land on the Long Beach side of Terminal Island for the price of one dollar! This land is the site for the naval shipyard now under construction.

The ironic twist to all of this political arm-twisting is that the new naval station will be called, "Naval Operating Base, Los Angeles."

Opposite: Shipboard scenes such as this will become commonplace in Long Beach, today named Pacific Fleet headquarters.

Douglas Plant Joins "Arsenal of Democracy"

(1941, October 18) Welcomed with the cheers of thousands of onlookers and well-wishers, the Douglas Aircraft plant was officially dedicated yesterday. Overhead a Douglas B-19's four 2,000-horsepower engines roared over the crowd as the world's largest bomber appeared out of nowhere to speed across the field at a scant 200 feet.

The new Long Beach facility is the latest of America's weapons and manufacturing plants to join President Roosevelt's "Arsenal of Democracy." As the B-19 made it apparently clear to all in attendance, the Douglas operation is ready to provide democracies around the world with the most

Douglas Aircraft's new Long Beach facility was officially dedicated yesterday.

55

technologically advanced aircraft to combat tyranny and warmongers.

The $12-million plant is part of the United States' National Defense Expansion Program and was financed and built by the U.S. Army. Douglas Aircraft was selected by the government to operate the plant after a review of several aircraft manufacturers. The plant will have the responsibility of exclusively producing military aircraft for use by America's allies.

The plant is unique in that it is the first "super blackout" aircraft manufacturing facility. It is completely invisible from the air at night, with light traps at all entrances. Douglas officials claim that a person would be unable to see the building even if standing a few yards away from it at nighttime.

The 1.4 million square feet of covered area will be fully lit by artificial lighting and will boast the largest air-conditioning system on the West Coast. All utilities have back-up safeguards, and the buildings are spaced so that in the event of a bomb attack the damage to adjacent structures will be minimized.

Douglas' Administration Center, a three-story, windowless building, is one of the largest of its type and the first constructed west of the Mississippi.

At the dedication ceremonies, it was hailed as the "world's most modern aircraft plant." Emphasizing the role that the plant will play in the "Arsenal of Democracy," Douglas President Donald Douglas told the assembled crowd, "America aroused is America united, and America united is America invincible."

Japanese to be Removed From Terminal Island

(1942, Spring) The school year is not quite out, but some of the students of San Pedro schools will be ending the year earlier than their friends will. For many of these students, there will be no senior proms, no graduations, and certainly no grad night parties.

In the wake of the Japanese attack on Pearl Harbor, an Executive Order, Number 9066, issued by President Roosevelt on February 19, designates military areas where military commanders can exclude civilian populations. The order further authorizes the building of "relocation camps" for those persons excluded. The effect of this order will be to remove all persons of Japanese ancestry from the West Coast of the United States.

For most of the Japanese students attending schools here, they and their families will be ordered to leave their homes, businesses, most of their possessions, and even their pets, and report to a temporary assembly center at Santa Anita racetrack. There they will be housed until they are assigned to one of 10 permanent concentration camps for the duration of the war with Japan.

Government officials believe that most of the Japanese from Terminal Island will eventually be held at a camp named Manzanar, which is being built outside of the small town of Independence in the desert foothills of the eastern Sierras. Manzanar is the first of the camps to be built and is approximately 200 miles north of Los Angeles.

Other camps slated for holding the Japanese will also be built at isolated sites well removed from populous cities. The War Relocation Authority has stated that in addition to Manzanar, the nine other camps will be located in Arizona, Utah, Wyoming, Colorado, Idaho, Arkansas, and California.

It is anticipated that Manzanar will eventually hold 10,000 people. Many of the younger Japanese who will go to the camps were born in America; and, in fact, it is estimated that the majority of internees at Manzanar will be U.S. citizens.

The U.S. Army, which is coordinating the removal, estimates that by the end of summer approximately 112,000 persons of Japanese ancestry on the West Coast will have been relocated.

PT. FERMIN LIGHTHOUSE GOES DARK

(1942) Spurred by fears of an ocean attack against the coast, the Coast Guard has ordered that the light of the Pt. Fermin lighthouse be turned off.

Additionally, the government has decided to paint the venerable landmark an olive green color to make it less conspicuous. The lighthouse has traditionally been painted a bright white.

The lighthouse has been in operation since 1874 when the lumber and bricks for the building were brought around the Horn by sailing vessels. The need for a lighthouse at the tip of the Palos Verdes Peninsula was recognized by the maritime leader of the time, and a government allocation of $4,000 was set aside in 1858 for the light's construction.

The New England-style lighthouse was originally equipped with a 2,100-candlelight oil lamp mounted inside of its cola. In 1925 a powerful 6,000-candlelight electric light replaced the oil lamps. The new light now boasts a range of 18 miles out to sea.

The Point Fermin Lighthouse, pictured here shortly before the war, has been ordered dark by the Coast Guard due to fears of an ocean attack against the coast.

"Rosie the Riveter" Sends Planes Off to War

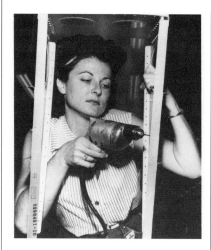

Female defense plant employees work an average of 8 to 10 hours a day, 6 days a week, at a starting pay rate of 60 cents an hour.

(1943) If America's success in the war is ever gauged by the forces on the homefront, then history will surely designate the women defense plant workers as heroes in the truest sense.

With the shortage of labor already at a critical stage, it is the women of America who have stepped forward to keep democracy's arsenal operating at a peak level. Performing jobs that were, until recently, done only by men,

the women have proven themselves to be equal to the challenge. And, on the jobs that require dexterity and detailed work, the women workers complete the tasks with a higher degree of accuracy.

In the Douglas Aircraft plant alone, women already comprise more than 85 percent of the work force. Nationally, it is estimated that nearly 19 million women will soon be employed by defense firms. Southern California, because of its concentration of aircraft plants, employs nearly 40 percent of these women.

Celebrated in song and fashion as "Rosie the Riveter," these women are breaking new ground in employment and social relationships. Women from different parts of the country have moved here and are working in Southern California. And the real "Rosies" are a mix of whites, blacks, Latins, single women, married women, and divorcees. From 18 to 60 and from all walks of life, all of the Rosies are keeping the pressure on the enemy by rolling out the warplanes needed overseas.

Many of the women have never

worked outside of their homes before, and not a small number have come to enjoy their new-found careers. A good number of the women have indicated that they would consider continuing to work in the plants even after the war ends.

Of course, many of the women are

also mothers and homemakers. Thus the plants are not without a good amount of absenteeism and resignations. However,

Below: Rosie the Riveter works diligently at her job. **Opposite:** Riveting airplane frames has suddenly become a female occupation as the war rages on.

at Douglas and other plants, these situations are being addressed.

In-plant shopping and banking services have dramatically helped to stabilize the labor force. The federal government is also doing its share. It recently began to help the plants provide child-care services for the mothers on the payroll.

Even the department store retailers have joined in the war effort. Buffum's, the fashionable department store in Long Beach, recently unveiled a new line of clothes especially for the woman plant worker. The "Victorall" one-piece coverall sells for $3.95; the zippered "Coverall" retails for $5.95, and the two-piece pants suit for plant or lounge wear also sells for $5.95.

But any of the true-life Rosies will be the first to admit that their careers are not the most glamorous ones. Despite the fashions, magazine articles, and photo stories, work in the plants is hard and hours are long.

Artificial lighting puts a strain on the eyes, air-conditioning is less than perfect, and the noise of the plant is unrelenting. The women work for 8 to 10 hours a day, 6 days a week, at a starting pay rate of 60 cents an hour. They have no sick leave, pension plans, or worker's compensation plans; plus, they are paid less than their male counterparts.

Yet the women continue their contributions to the war effort. Workers at the Douglas plant are capable of turning out 11 warplanes on a good day, and a large portion of the credit must be given to the "Rosies" of the plant.

Pedro Shipyards Humming

(1943, December) A better Christmas present from San Pedro shipyards to America's war effort couldn't have been asked for, nor given. As the country enters the third year of the conflict, the shipyards of San Pedro are rising to the occasion and going even further in helping to crush the Axis tyranny overseas.

All of the shipworks in San Pedro Bay are contributing to the shipbuilding and repair efforts. The smaller

yards are taking on the duties of building smaller, auxiliary craft and conducting essential repair jobs, while the larger companies are busy launching combat and cargo vessels.

Certainly one of the success stories of the war will be that of California Shipbuilding Corporation. With the assistance of the U.S. Maritime Commission, the company was formed by a group of experts in the field of large construction projects, such as refineries, dams, and bridges. It was felt that the expertise of these men could be transferred to the construction of ships.

In September 1941 the *John C. Fremont,* the first emergency cargo vessel, designated as EC-2s or better known as "Liberty" ships, rolled down the quays into the waters of Cerritos Channel. This was the first delivery on an initial contract for 55 such Liberty ships that Calship had with the Maritime Commission. Several contracts later, Calship is now employing 40,000 people to meet those deadlines.

The ships, which will be manned by U.S. Merchant Marines, will serve in all theaters of the war. The vessels are 427 feet in length with a beam of 57 feet and a cargo capacity of 468,000 cubic feet. A crew of 37 will man each Liberty. A newer, better-designed version of the ships, designated the V-1 or

Left: Another Liberty ship slides down the ways at Calship, one of the nation's most productive wartime shipyards. Opposite: Some of Calship's 40,000 employees recently gathered for a wartime rally.

Victory ship, is now being built by the San Pedro yards. Each of the vessels carries a price tag of $1.65 million. Thus the Calship contract is worth $93 million to the company.

This month saw Calship deliver its 196th Liberty ship of the year. Twenty-three ships were delivered in this month alone. All of this activity translates into the amazing rate of one Liberty ship being launched by Calship every 46.5 hours.

But Calship is only one of the heroes of the shipbuilding effort. Consolidated Steel Company is also on a breakneck schedule with its launching of Liberty ships and troop carriers. Bethlehem Steel is working overtime building destroyers and converting cargo vessels to troop carriers. Harbor Boat Works has its hands full delivering destroyers, sub chasers, and PT boats. Western Pipe and Steel, Los Angeles Shipbuilding and Drydock Company, and Craig Shipyards are others making significant contributions to bring an end to the hostilities.

With the construction schedules and procedures fully operational, some naval experts predict that yards like Calship and Consolidated will be able to produce hundreds of ships every year. Indeed, the assembly line techniques allow for 12 or more ships to be worked on simultaneously.

And so the welders' torches will continue to sparkle in the night sky, and the riveters' chatter will sound throughout the day. And surely, like the men on the front lines, the San Pedro shipyards will be in it for the duration.

Gun Batteries Deactivated

(1944) Fort MacArthur's huge coastal artillery gun batteries, guardians of the bay for nearly 30 years, have been ordered deactivated. The three batteries, located on the Upper Reservation of the Army post, were installed to defend the coast and harbor of San Pedro Bay. Each of the three batteries is named in honor of two Army generals. Construction of the emplacements began in 1914 and was completed in 1917.

Batteries Osgood-Farley and Merriam-Leary both house paired 14-inch disappearing rifles, which are typical of the harbor and coastal defense weaponry of the time. The cannon are mounted in bunkers below ground level to reduce their visibility to the enemy. Only when the gun carriages raised the weapons into firing position would they be visible. After a round was fired, the recoil of the gun would force the carriage to lower.

The Barlow-Saxton battery, located higher up on the Reservation, consists of two emplacements, each housing four 12-inch tube mortars.

Construction of the batteries began after Congress passed a $886,800 appropriation for the fortification and defense of San Pedro in January 1914. The batteries are huge underground systems of powder and storage rooms, fire control centers, generator rooms, tunnels, and air galleries. A network of truckways and access roads connect the batteries. The front walls of the gun emplacement are 20 feet thick, and the roof of the main structure is 9 feet thick and covered with 10 feet of earth.

An Army spokesman said that increased antiaircraft and antisubmarine activities will assume the defense of the coast and harbor. A drawback of the large weapons is the limited range of their shells due to the use of the disappearing carriage design. Further, because of their permanent placement facing the sea, they are vulnerable to attack from the rear.

The Army will remove the weapons upon official deactivation, but the emplacements will remain.

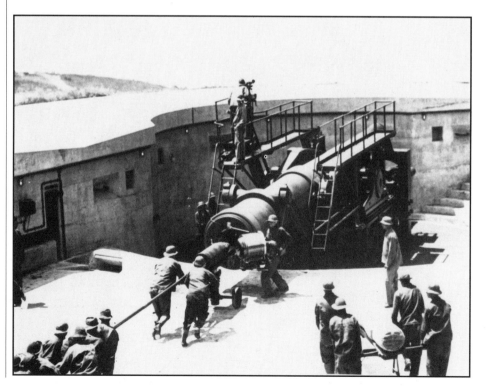

Left: Fort MacArthur's big guns have been ordered silenced. Opposite: Fort MacArthur is named for Arthur MacArthur, father of General Douglas MacArthur.

"Herman the German" Comes to Naval Shipyard

L.A. Harbor—Nation's Leading Fishing Port

A "Queen" Arrives in Long Beach

Oil Company to Build Islands

Vincent Thomas Bridge Opens

Harbor Floating on Oil...and Sinking

Critics Eat Crow as "Goose" Flies

JFK Assassinated in Dallas

First U.S. Manned Flight

Lakewood Opts for Incorporation

Port Officials Woo Japan Auto Maker

Subsidence Plan Adopted

Gambling Ship Cashes in

Containerized Cargo Makes Debut

Chapter 5

Peace and Prosperity

(1946-1967)

SAN PEDRO BAY		THE NATION	
1946	"Herman the German" comes to Naval Shipyard (p. 66)	1950	U.S. population is 150.6 million
1946	Gambling ship commodore cashes in chips (p. 67)	1950	U.S. forces sent to Korea
1947	Critics eat crow as "Goose" flies (p. 68)	1951	First transcontinental television broadcast
1950	Harbor floating on oil. . . and sinking (p. 69)	1953	Korean Conflict ends
1954	Lakewood opts for incorporation (p. 70)	1953	Congress enacts Civil Rights Act
1958	Subsidence plan adopted (p. 71)	1960	U.S. population is 179.3 million
1958	L.A. Harbor–Nation's leading Fishing Port (p. 71)	1960	John F. Kennedy elected President
1962	Containerized cargo makes debut (p. 72)	1961	Alan Shepard makes first U.S. manned space flight
1963	Vincent Thomas Bridge opens (p. 73)	1962	John Glenn orbits earth
1964	Port officials woo Japan auto makers (p. 76)	1962	Cuban missile crisis
1965	Oil Companies to build islands (p. 76)	1963	JFK assassinated in Dallas
1967	A "Queen" arrives in Long Beach (p. 77)	1964	Civil Rights Act of 1964
		1964	U.S. planes bomb North Vietnam
		1965	President Johnson sends U.S. troops to Vietnam

"Herman the German" Comes to Naval Shipyard

(1946, November) In the annals of war and reparations, money, jewels, castles, armaments, lands, titles, and people have passed from vanquished to victor. Now, we have another item to add to the list. The world's largest self-propelled floating crane, a war prize from Germany, ended the journey to its new home, the Long Beach Naval Shipyard.

Nicknamed "Herman the German," the crane is actually one of four cranes the Germans built in 1941 at Bremerhaven at a cost of $3.5 million. One crane was captured by the British and the third by the Russians. The fourth crane was sunk by the Allies at Hamburg.

As the British attempted to move their crane across the English Channel, the top-heavy craft capsized and sunk during a storm.

Having the benefit of that episode, the Americans partially disassembled the crane for its trip back to the states. The 264-foot main boom, counterweight, and deck superstructures were removed to make the move easier. The pontoon section of the crane was piloted across the Atlantic and through the Panama Canal by U.S. Navy personnel.

Prior tests of the crane list its capacity at 425 tons, with a lifting capability of 386 tons. In Long Beach, the crane, now officially designated the YD-171, will be used for heavy lifting and special moves in the shipyard. It will undergo re-rigging and extensive tests before being put back in operation. Navy officials estimate that it will be two years before "Herman" will be able to go to work for the Navy.

"Herman the German," the world's largest self-propelled floating crane, is capable of lifting 386 tons.

Gambling Ship Commodore Cashes in Chips

(1946) Tony Cornero, long known as the "Commodore of the Gambling Fleet" has finally been forced to cash in his chips. His latest floating gaming ship, the *Lux,* has been seized by state officials and will soon be placed on the auction block. Spearheaded by

Cornero's longtime nemesis, Governor Earl Warren, the raid and subsequent seizure took place only three days after the ship opened for business. This was Cornero's latest gambling vessel operation and had already garnered $175,000 for its owner in its short lifespan.

Cornero began his "career" by running Scotch to the Southern California coast during the Prohibition years. His first involvement with gambling ships came in the early 1930s, when he entered into a partnership with the Blazer brothers, operating the *Tango*

off the Southern California coastline.

However, the first such gambling ship off the coast of Southern California was the *Johana Smith,* which began operating in 1929. So popular was the ship with local gamblers, that crowds of 50,000 a week were not

The *Rex* was the most lavish of Tony Cornero's gambling ships.

uncommon.

Owners of such ships made sure that they anchored at least three miles away from the shoreline, safely beyond California's jurisdiction. Patrons boarded water taxis on shore that carried them to the waiting vessels.

Once onboard, gamblers could try their luck at cards, roulette, craps, bingo, and slot machines, all available to help the player get rich quick or to part the player from his cash . . . usually, the latter.

Cornero ended his partnership with the Blazers but returned to the high seas in 1938 with what was to be the most lavish of the gambling fleet, the *Rex*. Not only did Cornero's ship offer the usual array of gaming tables, but it was also tastefully appointed with fine European furnishings and decor. And to further heighten the glamour, full floor shows were produced for the entertainment of the players.

To convince the authorities that his gambling operation was honest and strictly legal, Cornero even conferred with the FBI prior to opening the *Rex* to the public.

However, the end was soon in sight. In August 1939 state officials raided the *Showboat* and *Tango,* both anchored off Long Beach. Cornero's *Rex* was located off of Santa Monica, but he refused to allow officers on board. Using high-pressure water hoses as weapons, the *Rex's* crew held the police at bay for nine days before Cornero finally surrendered.

The war and mounting legal skirmishes exacted their toll on the ship's operators, until the Commodore's most recent attempt at a comeback was mounted.

Registering the *Lux* as a coastal trading ship, Cornero anchored her off of Long Beach. Governor Warren, looking for a way to end the gambling ships once and for all, raided the *Lux,* stating that the ship was neither involved in trade nor was it traveling coastwise.

Regardless of one's position toward gambling, with the last of the floating gaming ships taken out of commission, a colorful and exciting chapter of California's history also comes to a close.

Critics Eat Crow as "Goose" Flies

(1947, November 3) Congressional critics of industrialist Howard Hughes and his "Spruce Goose" were summarily silenced yesterday over the waters of Long Beach harbor.

With the controversial Hughes at the controls, the huge eight-engine HK-1 *Hercules* lifted off during what was supposed to have been merely a test run on the harbor's waters. The entire flight covered a distance of about one mile at a height of 85 feet.

Critics of Hughes and the all-wood airplane have become more vocal over the last several years. Led by Senator Owen Brewster of Maine, they questioned whether the flying boat would ever fly, or even more pointedly,

whether it could fly. It was during one of Brewster's congressional hearings that Hughes was accused of bilking the government of millions of dollars and of bribing officials to obtain federal contracts.

In the increasingly acrimonious battle between Hughes and Brewster, the owner of Hughes Tool Company and Trans World Airlines revealed that Brewster had flown to California and asked Hughes to merge TWA with Pan American Airways. In exchange Brewster would call off his investigation of Hughes.

Retorting to this accusation, Brewster denounced the flying boat as a "lumberyard" boondoggle that

To the amazement of its Congressional critics, Howard Hughes' *Hercules* took to the air yesterday over Long Beach harbor.

would never fly.

Ironically, it was the U.S. government that spawned the birth of the HK-1. America was suffering large losses of men and material to German U-Boat attacks on troop transport ships during the early part of the war. Looking to find a safe and fast way to move troops across the Atlantic, the U.S. War Production Board awarded a $60-million contract to the Kaiser-Hughes Corporation for the construction of three troop transport flying boats in 1942. Because of the scarcity of metal, the specifications called for the plane to be built entirely of wood. However, two years later, the threat of U-Boat attacks diminished with the increased use of antisubmarine aircraft and destroyers with depth charges. Kaiser pulled out of the venture, but Hughes decided to continue it by adding $7.2 million of his own money to finish building the plane.

When the plane was still not completed at the end of the war, Brewster and his colleagues began to doubt Hughes' ability to deliver the airplane, and thus began their investigations.

The aircraft itself is not made of a single piece of spruce. The skin of the ship is constructed of laminated and bonded plywood, and birch is used extensively throughout. Its wings are 11.5 feet thick and span 320 feet from tip to tip. Each of the propellers stands 17 feet tall and is attached to a 3,000-horsepower Pratt & Whitney engine. Its troop-carrying capacity is 750 troops or a payload of 130,000 pounds. The plane is also designed to act as a 350-bed hospital. These specifications make the HK-1 the world's largest airplane.

According to a source close to Hughes, he sent a telegram to Senator Brewster once the flight was completed. The message read, "There, Brewster, the s.o.b. flies."

Harbor Floating on Oil...and Sinking

(1950) The first oil wells came to the port in 1938. And, as earlier wells brought prosperity and delivered huge deposits to the city coffers, so did those in the harbor.

In 1943 the Long Beach Oil Development Company, the city's chief oil producer, was operating 126 wells and pumping 17,000 barrels of petroleum a day and generating $10 million annually for Long Beach.

However, two years prior to that, a small tarnish on this rosy picture began to emerge. Geologic surveys of Terminal Island revealed that certain portions near the Navy's installation had actually sunk 1.3 feet.

In 1945 a U.S. Coast and Geodetic Survey showed that east Terminal Island had sunk 4.2 feet between 1931 and 1945. The evidence was mounting that the cause of this subsidence was none other than the extraction of oil from the rich East Wilmington Oil Field on which the Port of Long Beach sits.

Additional surveys and reports indi-

Above: The sinking harbor has put this canine's favorite hydrant well out of reach. Left: Subsidence in the harbor due to extensive pumping of oil has caused severe flooding.

cate that the subsidence is centered in an oblong bowl in the area of the Southern California Edison generating plant. The longer axis runs northwest to southeast for approximately six miles; the shorter northeast to southwest axis is about four miles in length. The plant itself has already sunk nearly 20 feet.

The effects of the subsidence can be seen throughout the harbor. Cracked foundations on structures, flooding of low-lying areas, twisted rail lines, and cracked roadways abound. Beneath the surface broken concrete water and sewer pipes are everywhere, and oil well pipes are twisted and bent, preventing oil from flowing from those wells.

Harbor Department efforts to stem the damage have only been remedial up until this time. Structures are built on higher ground and retaining walls and dikes are heightened, but a solution to the problem is yet to be found. A Harbor Department consultant, Dr. Frank S. Hudson, has ominously warned that if nothing is done to stop the subsidence, the land will continue sinking to a level of minus 72 feet.

And, if this is not enough of a problem to the city, the Navy has also indicated that they are considering closing their shipyard because of the sinking. With it would go the 6,500 jobs that it provides, the $31-million annual payroll, and the $127 million that is circulated in the area because of the yard's activities.

Ironically, the bounty of the city's oil boom has turned into a nightmare of epic proportions.

Lakewood Opts for Incorporation

(1954, March) Lakewood will not be Long Beach! Ending years of speculation over the fate of the mushrooming community northeast of Long Beach, residents of Lakewood Village have decided to incorporate as California's newest city. The vote puts an end to earlier discussions about whether the city of Long Beach would annex the boomtown suburb.

Ever since the opening of the Douglas Aircraft plant in north Long Beach in 1940, new real estate developments have sprouted in the area. In 1941, 1,100 new homes were built in the vicinity of Lakewood, extending Long Beach's northern boundary.

However, it was not until 1950 that Lakewood really entered into its present fast-growth mode.

The Lakewood Park Corporation, consisting of developers Mark Taper, Ben Weingart, and Lou Boyar, purchased 3,400 acres of land from the Montana Land Company for $8.8 million. The corporation's plan was to build 17,500 homes in the span of 18 months. With the need for housing for Douglas employees, returning veterans, and newcomers to Southern California, the time seemed right for Taper and his partners.

With the slogan for the new enterprise, "The City as New as Tomorrow," Lakewood soon became the world's largest planned community and the fastest-growing city in the

Upon incorporation, Lakewood, with 70,000 residents, will become California's sixth-largest city.

United States.

The project entails 380 miles of streets, 340 miles of sanitary sewers, and 5,000 streetlights. Twenty schools, 37 playgrounds, and 17 churches are also part of the development. Even the Lakewood Shopping Center was included when the original plans were first drawn.

Each of the two- or three-bedroom homes sits on a 50-foot by 100-foot lot with a one- or two-car garage. Prices were set at from $7,825 to $9,700. Veterans utilizing the G.I. Bill could move in with no down payment, while others paid a one-third down payment. Monthly payments are $43 to $54, including taxes, insurance, and interest.

The homes were built utilizing concepts taken from mass manufacturing. Teams of 30 workers moved throughout the tracts to an individual home site, where they were met by pre-cut lumber. Foundation excavations took only 15 minutes. Each worker possessed a specific skill and used it on every house on which he worked. As supply trucks passed by a home under construction, a conveyor belt stretched out to the rooftop where a load of shingles was delivered to the waiting roofers. Every home is equipped with a garbage disposal unit located under the sink. In fact, promotional brochures for the homes stated that Lakewood would be America's first garbage-free city.

Lakewood's population now stands at 70,000 and upon its formal incorporation it will become California's sixth-largest city.

Subsidence Plan Adopted

(1958) A plan to halt the sinking of the Port of Long Beach has been adopted by the state. The California Subsidence Act of 1958 has been signed into law after prolonged meetings and hearings on the subject.

The act is seen as essential for the City of Long Beach to halt the alarming rate of subsidence that has wreaked havoc on its port since the 1940s. The act grants Long Beach the power of eminent domain to conduct mandatory repressurization of oil wells whenever it is required to stop further sinking within the harbor.

Repressurization of the East Wilmington Oil Field under the port is seen to be the best method to halt the subsidence caused by the extraction of petroleum. Repressurizing is accomplished by injecting water back into the wells, thereby stabilizing the surface of the land.

Water injection methods were first used in oil fields in Texas and Louisiana. The resulting repressurization of the wells also increased their useful lives after primary drilling was no longer effective in extracting oil.

In 1953 an experimental water injection well was built by the Harbor Department as a test project. With only a minimal amount of injection, stabilization was achieved in only a few months.

In Long Beach a unitized process of repressurization is required because of the bowl-shaped depression that exists as a result of subsidence. Water must be injected to an entire area or zone and not only into individual wells. To do otherwise would result in some wells being flooded while others would benefit by more oil being pushed into their wells. A side benefit of repressurization is, of course, the additional oil that will be available for extraction.

In order to accomplish this task, benchmark readings will be taken on a regular basis. If movement is detected over several readings, then the appropriate well will be injected to compensate for the movement. It is hoped that this fine-tuning process will finally put a stop to the sinking of the port.

L.A. Harbor—Nation's Leading Fishing Port

(1958) Los Angeles Harbor, already a world leader in commercial shipping, has also retained its crown as America's leading fishing and canning harbor.

Tuna and mackerel catches again led all species that were unloaded and processed at the port's Fish Harbor commercial fishing facility. A total of 354.4 million tons of fish valued at $25.4 million led all other fishing ports in the country.

Purse seiners were utilized as the predominant method of catching the tuna. Forty-two such ships (down from last years' 60 vessels) worked to net the various deep-sea longfins.

By September 30, 348 million pounds of tuna had already been netted. The past year was an especially good year for bluefin tuna with a total haul of 30 million pounds. In all of California, 366 million pounds of tuna were brought into port by that date.

Imports of foreign tuna again rose. By October 1, 84 million pounds of the fish was brought into San Pedro canneries. Most of the tuna was from Japan.

The harbor's canneries also maintained their leadership as the world's largest canning and processing center with 9.4 million cases of tuna packed, while in the entire United States 11.9 million cases of tuna were canned.

The annual payroll of the canneries topped $15 million for the more than 5,000 people whose livelihoods depend on the processors. The processed, canned fish from San Pedro entered the stream of commerce with a total value of $150 million. Throughout the harbor, millions were spent in the entire fishing industry, with investments totaling $275 million pumped into the local economy by commercial fishermen, processors, and the Harbor Department.

Containerized Cargo Makes Debut

(1962, September 24) A new era in intercoastal shipping was heralded today with the arrival of the SS *Elizabethport* at the Port of Long Beach. The vessel called at the new five-acre combination truck and container terminal that the Port built for the Sea Land Service Company.

Shipping by containers is a revolutionary system of cargo transportation. Goods are placed in a weatherproof, secured, 35-foot-long metal container that is sealed at the point of loading. The containers are then trucked to a waiting vessel where they are lifted directly off the truck beds and onto a predetermined spot on the ship. Only when the container reaches its final destination is it opened.

This seemingly simple concept of cargo movement is the brainchild of Malcom McLean, the chairman of Sea Land Industries. Formerly the president of his own trucking company, McLean went on to form the Pan Atlantic Steamship Company in 1956. The first such movement of containers took place in April of that year, when a converted T-2 World War II tanker was specially outfitted to carry 58 containers from New Jersey to Houston, Texas.

Sea Land's new service will start with two vessels calling at Long Beach every 18 days. In the second year four jumbo "trailerships" will increase the sailings to once every nine days.

Long Beach was selected by Sea Land for its new terminal because the port was willing to take a chance on the new technology of containerization. Other ports that were approached by McLean insisted on the traditional rate of $.80 per ton of cargo unloaded. With the increased efficiency that containers offer, that rate would result in uneconomically high rates.

By breaking with tradition, Long Beach is willing to give Sea Land a flat rental rate for its new operation. While that policy may not sit well with other ports, officials at Long Beach believe that the new mechanization of the industry demands that new ways of doing business must also be found to keep up with those changes.

Long Beach harbor's first containerized cargo has arrived, signaling a new era in intercoastal shipping.

Vincent Thomas Bridge Opens

(1963, November 15) A new institution, bright green and rising 385 feet into the morning haze, greeted San Pedro residents today, as the Vincent Thomas Bridge opened with the first cars streaming across its four lanes of pavement.

Named after the longtime legislator from the 52nd Assembly District, the bridge marks the culmination of a 20-year fight by Thomas to connect Terminal Island with San Pedro.

Thomas first proposed a two-lane tunnel to run under the main channel of the Port of Los Angeles. This initial concept was soon changed to a four-lane bridge that would span the entire channel. Critics of the plan soon began calling it the "bridge to nowhere," saying that nothing would come of it.

Thomas persevered through 3 governors and 16 pieces of legislation to get the necessary funds allocated for his plan. Today, the 6,060-foot bridge stands as the third-largest suspension bridge in the state and the tallest

Assemblyman Vincent Thomas, for whom the bridge is named, fought for 20 years to connect San Pedro with Terminal Island.

structure in the South Bay.

The bridge is the first of its kind to be built on piles rather than on concrete supports. Each of the piles is manufactured to support 145 tons.

The main suspension cables are 14 inches in diameter and designed to withstand winds of 90 miles per hour. An elaborate weaving of 4,028 strands of galvanized wires into 19 cables of 212 wires each makes up the main cable. The cable is then fully encased and strung between the support arms.

The bridge will be under the jurisdiction of the Toll Bridge Authority of the State of California, and a 25-cent toll will be charged each way. The tolls will go toward paying for the $22-million bridge.

Maintenance of the bridge, including the non-stop painting, will be conducted by the California Department of Transportation. The special anti-corrosion green paint is a formula devised by the department and will not harm the waters below it should it drip while painting. Transportation officials say that it will take 20 years to fully paint the bridge; then the job will start over again.

While the bridge marks an exciting new phase for the harbor, it also spells doom for another port institution. The venerable ferry service from the foot of Sixth Street to the Ferry Building on Terminal Island ceases operation with the opening of the bridge.

According to state law, ferries are forbidden to operate on waterways when they would compete with state-owned toll bridges.

The new 6,060-foot Vincent Thomas Bridge connects Terminal Island and San Pedro

Port Officials Woo Japan Auto Makers

(1964) Port of Long Beach officials recently returned from a trade mission to Japan, where they visited two automakers. Led by Port General Manager Charles Vickers, the port delegation met with the Japanese automakers and discussed the possible location of their import facilities in Long Beach.

The importation of foreign automobiles is a growing segment of the port's list of commodities entering the country. Nearly 40,000 foreign cars are presently being imported through the port. The initial shipments started in the early 1950s with the popular Jaguar, Triumph, and MG cars from Great Britain. However, by the early 1960s, the leader by far was the German-built Volkswagen. With the VW seen almost everywhere on our streets, it is easy to understand that 25,268 of the "beetles" came through the port last year.

The Port officials went to Japan with the hopes of interesting Japanese car manufacturers in establishing permanent facilities in Long Beach through which to import their cars. A small number of Toyota automobiles had been brought to the port in the past. However, because of a lack of trained service mechanics, many of the cars went unsold for long periods of time.

The Japanese automakers had an inconspicuous start in Long Beach several years ago. Testing the auto sales waters for the first time in America, the Toyota automobile company sent two of its vehicles to the U.S. in 1957 via the Port of Long Beach.

Oil Companies to Build Islands

(1965) A consortium of five oil companies has been selected by the city of Long Beach to conduct the development of the newly announced East Wilmington Oil Field. The group, to be called THUMS (for Texaco, Humble, Union, Mobil, and Shell), will have the exclusive right to oil production of the oil-rich lands east of the existing Wilmington Oil Field.

As part of the deal, Long Beach is insisting that the five companies build artificial islands in the harbor from which to base their operations. The firms have resisted this stipulation from the onset, but the city has maintained the requirement throughout the negotiations. The message is clear. "If you want to drill, it will be from oil islands."

As part of the construction plans, aesthetic and environmental considerations are to be major factors in the final design of the islands. The drilling rigs are to be shrouded in pastel-colored panels; trees will be planted; and a lighted waterfall will grace the island closest to the shoreline.

Each of the islands will be built in much the same way that the harbor has been built, by dredging and landfilling. Perimeter rock from Catalina Island will be laid from the ocean floor upwards. Then sand will be dredged and filled inside the perimeter, creating the new land.

All of the wells on the islands will be electrically powered or use subsurface hydraulic pumps. This will make for an unusually quiet oil production operation and will allow the islands to retain a natural appearance.

Fifty thousand feet each of communications and electrical power wire will be needed to connect the islands with the mainland. One hundred forty thousand feet of steel pipeline will be installed to transport the oil to the waiting refineries. The pipelines will be specially coated to guard against corrosion, and anti-corrosive chemicals will be pumped throughout the lines to help maintain their integrity. To further guard against an accidental spill, periodic electronic inspection of the pipelines will be conducted to locate areas of potential damage.

Each of the islands will cost $2 million to build, with another one million dollars for beautification work. However, the return to THUMS will also be great. The value of the oil field is estimated to be $3 billion, with a total field production of 1.2 billion barrels of oil and 234 billion cubic feet of natural gas.

A "Queen" Arrives in Long Beach

(1967, December 10) Amid a flotilla of small craft, blaring ships' whistles, and the cheers of thousands of spectators, Long Beach's new "Queen" yesterday entered the city of her future residence.

The R.M.S. *Queen Mary,* the historic luxury ocean liner of the Cunard Line, steamed majestically into Long Beach harbor to signal what is hoped by the city fathers to be the start of a revitalization of the downtown shoreline.

The decision to bring the *Queen Mary* to Long Beach began more than a year ago with Harbor Commissioner H.E. "Bud" Ridings. When Cunard announced that the *Queen* was up for sale, Ridings tried to interest the private travel industry in taking on the ship.

When that proposal was rejected, the City of Long Beach took it upon itself to enter the bidding for the ship. On July 26 of this year, Cunard elected to accept the city's bid of $3.45 million. Officials at the line's headquarters said that one of the compelling reasons for accepting Long Beach's bid was the fact that the City's plans would ensure that the character of the *Queen Mary* would be preserved.

Those plans call for a maritime

The *Queen Mary* received a regal welcome as she sailed into Long Beach harbor.

museum to be built on the ship as well as operating the vessel as a hotel and entertainment attraction. Long Beach's tourism industry has been lagging for many years, and the purchase of the *Queen* is seen as a way to reverse the slide. A new city department has been created for the purpose of administering the ship's operation.

Initial estimates call for refurbishing costs to run from $2 million to $5 million and for the job to take approximately three years. All of the work will be done on the west end of the harbor. After that the ship will be brought to a site on the east end of the port, where she will be permanently berthed.

On her final voyage to Long Beach, 1,200 passengers joined the ship on the 15,000-mile journey around Cape Horn. Even though they were participating in history, many of the passengers complained of poor service and lack of air-conditioning, which made the tropical portions of the trip especially trying.

Ports and Cities Fight Offshore Airport Plan

Fishermen Squeezed by Foreign Fleets

Beacon Street to be Razed

Vietnam War Ends

Neil Armstrong is First Man to Walk on Moon

Tanker Blast Kills Five

San Pedro Bay–Nation's Leading Port Complex

Nixon Resigns

Spruce Emerges From Ne...

Ports Unveil 2020 Plan

DC-3 Celebrates 50th

Space Shuttle Challenger Explodes

World Trade Center Opens

Earthquake in L.A. Than One Billion D...

Endings and Beginnings

(1970s-1989)

Fishermen Squeezed by Foreign Fleets

(1972) Fishermen from San Pedro and ports up and down the coast are becoming more and more accustomed to the sight of large, modern fishing fleets flying the colors of Russia and Japan on the open ocean. Accompanied by huge, floating mother or factory ships, the fleets sweep through schools of fish raking in prodigious catches . . . catches that would previously be going into the nets of American ships.

It is widely acknowledged by the Americans that the modern ships and equipment of the Russians and Japanese far surpass the efficiency of U.S fleets. The foreign ships are generally faster, larger, and carry far more sophisticated instrumentation and processing capabilities.

The logical consequence of this is that it becomes harder and harder for American commercial fishermen to fill their holds with fish. Even more alarming is the fact that the richest fisheries are simply being overfished because of the increased fishing pressure exerted by the newcomers.

This depletion of fish schools has forced some San Pedro vessels to venture for months to distant fishing grounds such as Africa and the Western Pacific to fill their holds. Some Americans have even set up bases of operations in foreign ports where labor costs are lower.

Commercial fishing interests have long lobbied Congress for help in staving off the foreign competition. Most commonly, an extension of the territorial limit for protected fishing zones has been requested.

Even this is, however, not as clear-cut as it might seem. Tuna fishermen vocally champion this course of action, citing Mexico's 200-mile limit off of its shores as giving Mexican fishing interests undue advantage over other fishing nations.

On the other side of the same coin, salmon fishermen in Alaska and the Pacific Northwest oppose such sanctions. Persons fishing in those waters say that, whereas tuna are free-roaming fish, salmon always return to their native streams to spawn. To protect the salmon within a 200-mile range and not in the open ocean could possibly eliminate an entire year's crop of fish.

At present Japan and America have an agreement that prohibits Japanese harvesting of salmon west of the meridian, a line that runs roughly north to south between Russia and the Alaskan peninsula. Salmon fishermen fear that the imposition of the 200-mile limit would cause the Japanese to abandon that agreement. The Americans would like to see a ban on the taking of salmon on the open sea and limit the fishery to an area conforming to the continental shelf of the United States.

American fishing interests say that what is at stake is nothing less than the survival of an industry in the country. Pointing out the state of affairs that plagued Monterey, fishermen are quick to remind people that 30 years ago, the city was the fishing capital of the West Coast. However, once the sardine fishery was overfished, the once-flourishing industry faded away. Today the city has moved to transform Cannery Row into a tourist center, depending on boutique shops and restaurants to support the economy.

Beacon Street to be Razed

(1975) In its heyday it was known to be more sinful than San Francisco's Barbary Coast. Its bars and saloons were a common bond among the seamen who sailed the oceans. To some, it was a home where friendships were nurtured and where people looked out for each other. But, recently, in the eyes of civic leaders, Beacon Street had simply become an eyesore and an embarrassment to San Pedro. It had become the town's skid row.

At one time it was a colorful, albeit tough, slice of a waterfront town. It possessed its own unique identity and, to some, a certain charm and appeal that could be found nowhere else. Today, all of that is replaced by cheap wine, trash, and alcoholism. But even this is due to change soon.

The Los Angeles Community Redevelopment Agency, infused with fresh funds from the federal government, will soon begin to raze the entire area. The 60-acre site, from 3rd to 7th streets and Harbor Boulevard to Mesa Street, will become the heart of a new, revitalized San Pedro.

Ever since the days when ships sailed on the wind, Beacon Street was a magnet for sailors on leave in San Pedro. Throughout their journeys seamen swapped tales about the good times that could be had on Beacon Street. They all knew the saloons in the area: the Pepper Tree, the Admiral Saloon, the Scuttlebutt Inn, the Silver Dollar, Lindskow's, the Bank Club, Tommy's, and Beacon Street's signature watering hole, Shanghai Red.

Originally the street was where the city's business district was located. By the 1920s the district started to move west onto Pacific Avenue, and more and more bars and saloons moved into the area. The Bank Club, one of the more famous of Beacon Street's bars, moved into an old bank building, hence, its name.

When the fleet dropped anchor, it was common to see the area filled with thousands upon thousands of thirsty sailors looking to blow off steam. Beacon's tattoo parlors, honky-tonk bars, and gambling establishments hummed with activity as did the hotels that rented rooms by the hour.

However, another institution as venerable as Shanghai Red was the Salvation Army band. Every Saturday night the band marched on Beacon Street, exhorting listeners to partake in more socially acceptable pastimes.

But with the coming of World War II also came elements of violence and crime. To those who lived and worked on the "Street," it had been a place where you could always be assured of being taken care of in times when you were pressed for money. People looked out for each other, and a sense of family existed. Then all of that began to change, and the area began its decline. And so it slid into its present condition. Ships have moved from canvas to computers, and San Pedro has grown to bypass the activities of Beacon Street.

Yet, with the passing of time, the tales get taller, the lights burn brighter, and the laughter is livelier. Beacon Street may be bowing to progress, but the spirit of the *Street* will always remain a part of San Pedro's history.

Tanker Blast Kills Five

(1976, December 18) A huge, fiery explosion on board an oil tanker berthed at the Port of Los Angeles killed five persons early last evening. Seven persons are also listed as missing, and the injured toll stands at 49.

The Liberian tanker *Sansinena* was chartered to the Union Oil Company and was scheduled to depart the harbor at 11:30 p.m. The vessel was in the process of taking on fuel when she was rocked by the blast that split her in two. Earlier in the day the tanker had off-loaded her cargo of 512,000 barrels of oil from Indonesia.

The blast occurred at 7:40 p.m. when the all-Italian crew was seated for dinner. Most of the crewmen were thrown overboard by the force of the explosion, and many suffered severe burns.

The explosion was felt as far away as 40 miles, and many San Pedro homes and retail stores had their windows shattered. Harbor Division police reported some looting of stores and soon had the area cordoned off.

Initial investigations indicate that the blast may have been caused by an explosion of an oxygen welding tank on the dock. A 300-foot hole in the side of the *Sansinena* resulted in the fore and aft sections of the ship being blown 150 feet apart from each other.

The superstructure of the ship was completely ripped from the rest of the vessel and thrown onto the adjoining dock. Flying metal and debris caused many of the injuries to men working on the piers.

Spectacular flames leapt 1,000 feet into the night sky over the port. Two hundred firefighters from 40 engine companies battled the fires as they spread onto the adjacent wharves. The night-long fight was joined by four fireboats and two helicopters.

At the Ports o' Call Village a police

The explosion of the tanker *Sansinena* last evening blew the fore and aft sections of the ship 150 feet apart.

helicopter circled overhead, ordering people to evacuate immediately and warning them that the area was in great danger.

Fire Department investigators say that hydrocarbon gas had accumulated in the tanks of the *Sansinena* after the oil discharging had been completed. The gas, which is highly volatile, created an extremely dangerous condition on board the ship just prior to the fatal explosion.

Star Kist Cannery is World's Largest

(1977) To the list of San Pedro "firsts" and "largests" can be added yet another item. This time it is the world's largest cannery.

The Star Kist cannery, a longtime harbor institution since its founding in 1917, now lays claim to the title of busiest and largest fish-processing plant in the world.

Last year Star Kist's 2,300 workers canned 75,000 tons of tuna along with lesser amounts of mackerel, anchovies, and bonita. While most of the fish was processed for human consumption and pet food, some was ground into fish meal, fertilizer, and animal feed.

Star Kist tuna clippers range far into South American, African, and South Pacific waters for the prized long-distance fish. Anywhere from 140 to 2,000 tons in weight, the tuna ships are, for the most part, owned in some propor-

tion by Star Kist. The others are independent vessels under contract to the cannery.

During peak production runs, Star Kist produces one million cans of tuna a day, utilizing 10,000 gallons of vegetable oil. Each can of tuna is coded on its lid with the exact date and time of canning, as well as information about the name of the vessel that brought the fish to San Pedro.

Together with other canneries in San Pedro, such as Van Camp Seafood Company and Pan Pacific Fisheries, harbor canneries packed more than half of all canned fish in the United States.

Today the cannery that was started in 1917 by Martin J. Bogdonavich as the French Sardine Company is the harbor area's largest employer with an annual payroll of $30 million.

Star Kist's San Pedro cannery is the world's busiest and largest fish-processing plant.

Pike Passes into Mists of Memory

(1979, September) It is quite a contrast for an area that once entertained thousands of frolickers every day. It was an eight-block amusement zone that once was one of America's five largest. It was a place known as one of California's premier attractions and a destination for tourists from all parts of the country. It was an amusement park known as "The Walk of a Thousand Lights."

Today the Pike, the longtime Long Beach fun and amusement area, is reduced to a few concessions and rides that are pale impostors of their predecessors. And now the Pike is officially closed.

Since the turn of the century, the beachfront fun and entertainment area was the focal point for socializing and spending a day at the beach. No one could come to Long Beach without a visit to the Pike.

The amusement park had its start in 1902 when Charles R. Drake, a retired military man from Arizona, formed the Long Beach Bath House and Amusement Company. He quickly convinced the Pacific Electric Company to extend their Red Car lines into Long Beach. This was crucial for the success of the plan that Drake had in mind.

Drake's company built a warm saltwater plunge and bathhouse for visitors to the beach. These became the mainstays of the area and remained so for

more than 60 years.

Soon after, a roller skating rink, miniature railroad, and playground were added to the beachfront. It was at this time that talk first arose about a West Coast amusement zone that would compare to Coney Island. Although it is not clear where the name arose, a newspaper item in 1905 referred to the area as simply, "The Pike."

Throughout the years the Pike was always filled with the smells of hot dogs and hamburgers, popcorn, and cotton candy wafting through the salt air. Games of chance, shooting galleries, dance halls, and souvenir shops all sought the attention of passersby. But the roller coasters and the famous Looff Hippodrome will always be remembered as the stars of the boardwalk.

In 1911 Charles Looff brought his carousel operation to Long Beach and started a mainstay at the Pike. His elaborate, hand-carved horses sported cutglass jewels and real horsehair tails. These carousel animals are today highly sought-after collectibles.

The history of roller coasters at the Pike is one of bigger and better. The Pike spanned the lives of three coasters, with the first going into operation in 1907. After eight years the operators built an even larger racer in order to stave off competition from a new concessionaire who was considering building a roller coaster on the east side of the pier. The original operators dismantled their original coaster and then installed the new roller coaster, calling it the *Jackrabbit Racer.*

But the granddaddy of all roller coasters on the Pike was the famous

Cyclone Racer. It began operating on Memorial Day 1930, and its spindly framework became synonymous with the Long Beach skyline and the Pike for nearly 50 years. Crowds lined up throughout all hours it was in operation. And even at the midnight closing hour, people were still waiting for that one last ride, especially to experience the horrendous 85-foot vertical drop that drove the coaster to speeds of up to 60 miles per hour.

Like so much of the Pike, however, changing times and tastes soon cast a dark cloud over the festive atmosphere of the beach amusement zone. The *Cyclone Racer* was not immune from it all, and, on September 15, 1968, the famous coaster screamed along its tracks for the last time. By then, however, the roller coaster was only the latest in an ever-growing list of closures on the Pike. The year 1948 saw the removal of the Silver Spray Pier; Colonel Drake's landmark Bath House and Plunge gave way to progress in 1966; and the Municipal Auditorium and Band Stand followed the *Cyclone Racer* into memory in 1975.

A 1958 proposal to enclose part of the amusement zone and to charge an admission was never implemented, and with the advent of Disneyland and its followers, the Pike began its spiraling decline into history.

As more and more concessions closed, the tide of progress grew stronger and stronger. In place of the demolished Auditorium, Lagoon, and Rainbow Pier, arose the new Convention Center and Terrace Theater. And, where bathers once waded among the crashing surf, Shoreline Drive now winds its way along the water.

The Pike, pictured here in its heyday with the *Cyclone Racer* at right, is no more.

Ports and Cities Fight Offshore Airport Plan

(1980, September) San Pedro and Long Beach have not always agreed on matters throughout their histories. But, when confronted with a proposal to build an offshore airport in San Pedro Bay, both cities joined forces in vocal opposition to the plan.

The proposed airport is the subject of a study just released by the Southern California Association of Governments (SCAG). Citing the increasing concern by homeowners over noise pollution near airports and the crucial need for more air passenger facilities, the study considered 19 locations as a site for a new airport.

After extensive analyses, the SCAG aviation committee concluded that an air passenger facility off the shores of San Pedro and Long Beach was the "most feasible" of the locations studied.

Preliminary plans call for a 2,800-acre landfill to be built one and one-half miles seaward of the present federal breakwater that stretches across San Pedro Bay. Water depths at this point average 80 feet.

The man-made island/airport would be larger than Santa Barbara Island and require 430 million cubic yards of fill to complete. To give an idea of how much earth this is, consider that the total amount of material excavated from the Panama Canal was less than half of what would be needed for the airport.

SCAG's projections indicate that airline passenger traffic will rise 173 percent over 1978's level by 1995. By that time, 109 million passengers will be using Southern California's airports. If the offshore plan is put into operation, an additional 75 million vehicle trips will be made through the harbor area. The Long Beach Freeway will have to be improved and extended through the Port of Long Beach and out to the island.

The project would take 8 to 10 years to finish at a cost of $3.4 billion. Opponents say that this figure is unrealistically low, and that a true estimate of the cost is more likely $6.5 billion to $15 billion.

Port and city officials of both San Pedro and Long Beach also point out that the SCAG plan places the island directly over the line of the Palos Verdes Fault. Further, the site would severely hamper the movement of commercial vessels into and out of the ports.

Administratively, the proposed airport would pose interesting questions about the control and decision-making procedures to be used as the location contains several parcels owned individually by Los Angeles, Long Beach, and the State of California.

San Pedro and Long Beach oppose the construction of an offshore airport.

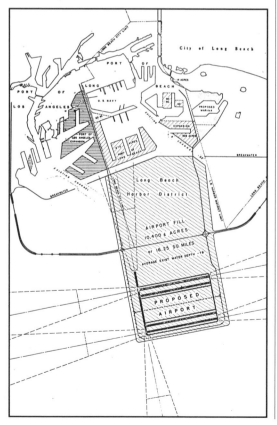

Spruce Goose Emerges from Nest

(1980, October 20) It was a tale passed on by word of mouth . . . A story of a fantastic object shrouded in the fog of mystery and speculation . . . A legend that existed and was embellished by the passage of time . . . But now, after 33 years in hiding, the mystery is finally revealed as the Howard Hughes' Flying Boat, the "Spruce Goose," was released from her berth of 37 years and allowed to feel the sunshine on her wings once more.

It was on November 2, 1947, that Howard Hughes, the recluse industrialist, piloted the HK-1 *Hercules* on its one and only flight over Long Beach Harbor. After the short one-mile flight, a special temperature-controlled hangar was built to house the aircraft on the west end of the Port of Long Beach.

With a Hughes guard always on duty, the world's-largest airplane remained hidden from the eyes of the public. Much as its owner became an object of curiosity and wonderment, so did the Spruce Goose.

Tales arose about Hughes arriving in the dead of night to fire up the engines. Stories grew about how Hughes passed on the edict that the plane must be kept in flight condition, regardless of cost. It was only when the landlords of the hangar, the Port of Long Beach, decided to locate a tanker terminal at the site, that thought was given to the eventual fate of the ship.

The plane is now in the ownership of the Summa Corporation, the holding company for all of the Hughes operations. Initial plans called for the aircraft to be cut into eight pieces and distributed to air museums throughout the country. A howl of protests from aircraft buffs and historians quickly forced another plan to be formulated.

As it now stands, the Spruce Goose will be donated to the Aero Club of Southern California, which will, in turn, loan it to the Wrather Corporation for permanent exhibition. The Wrather group intends to put the aircraft on public display adjacent to the *Queen Mary,* the world's-largest airplane next to the world's-largest ocean liner. Plans call for the construction of the world's-largest aluminum geodesic dome to house the Spruce Goose.

After being towed out of its hangar, the plane was lifted onto land by a huge floating crane. There she will rest for two years during the building of the dome. After that, another move by barge will take the giant flying boat to her place of permanent exhibition.

Tugboats slowly maneuver the 200-ton "Spruce Goose" down the Terminal Island channel toward her temporary home in the Port of Long Beach.

Ports Unveil 2020 Plan

(1984) In an unprecedented show of cooperation, the ports of Los Angeles and Long Beach have announced a 35-year master plan for the development of San Pedro Bay.

The joint study was submitted in response to a U.S. Army Corps of Engineers' request that the twin ports draw up a comprehensive blueprint for the future of the harbor complex. Staffs of both ports and the Corps cooperated to formulate the long-range planning document called the 2020 Plan.

Anchored by massive landfills that will encompass 2,600 acres, the project consists of four distinct phases of creation of new land areas by means of dredging and landfilling. The acreage will be roughly divided equally between the ports, which are already the West Coast's leading harbors in terms of tonnage moved and revenues generated.

The requirement of 2,600 acres is based on projections of cargo movements that were generated by economic models. It is estimated that by the year 2020, cargo tonnages passing through San Pedro Bay will triple to 223 million tons. In 1980 Long Beach and Los Angeles handled 83 million tons of cargo.

Without building any new terminals, the ports will be able to handle only 150 million tons of products in 2020. This means that the 73-million-ton shortfall would have to be diverted to other ports, resulting in lost revenues and jobs to the Southern California region.

The cost for the entire plan is set at $4 billion in 1983 dollars. Phase I is scheduled to be completed in 1992 and will result in 950 new acres of land. Phase II will be completed in 2002 and see 585 new acres created. The 399-acre Phase III is scheduled for a 2010 finish date. And the final phase will consist of 666 acres of landfill on the outside of the existing federal breakwater.

Immediate and tangible benefits of the project will be the dramatic increase in jobs that the construction and operation of new terminals will generate nationally. Port officials say that 779,800 job years or 21,000 new jobs per year of the project will be created across the nation.

This artist's conception shows how the harbor will look when 2,600 acres of landfill are added and the 2020 Plan is completed.

DC-3 Celebrates 50th

(1985) After 50 years of service, the DC-3 and its military version, the C-47, are undeniably the best-loved aircraft that ever rolled down an assembly plant line. From pilots of supersonic aircraft to arm-chair aviators, the DC-3 holds its admirers in a grip that only seems to grow stronger with the passing of time. DC-3 clubs are to be found throughout the world, and more books have been written about the DC-3 than about any other airplane, past or present.

The reasons for the lore and legend of the DC-3 are as varied as those who love the airplane. Maybe it was the plane in which many people had their first airplane ride. Or it may be the fact that the olive-drab C-47s are remembered as they glided over far-off airstrips in exotic locales dropping long-awaited supplies and letters from home to young troopers, true angels from the sky. Or, maybe yet, it simply reminds us of a time when it took 15 hours to fly from New York to Los Angeles, a time when life was slower and easier to comprehend.

The DC-3 made its debut in 1935 as the Douglas Sleeper Transport or DST/DC-3 as it was officially named by Douglas Aircraft designers. The third of the DC class of planes, the DST gained life in response to a request from American Airlines chief, C.R. Smith, for a sleeper version of Douglas' popular DC-2.

The fuselage of the DC-2 was widened, and a greater range and larger payload was built into the new craft. The DSTs carried 14 passengers and were fully outfitted for luxurious transcontinental travel. Upper berths retracted into the ceiling and lower berths were transformed into adjustable day coach chairs. A day version of the DC-3 allowed for a 100 percent increase in passenger capacity over the DC-2.

The first flight of the DC-3 took place on December 17, 1935. As it was only a test of a new model aircraft, not a single photographer was present to record what would become a historic flight.

So successful was the new passenger plane, that virtually all airlines queued up with orders for the DC-3. The impact of the airplane was such that it almost single-handedly made air passenger travel a profitable operation for airlines.

Within the first 10 years of production, 10,629 of the aircraft in both civilian and military configurations were produced at plants in Long Beach, Santa Monica, and Oklahoma City.

Manufacturing licenses were granted to Mitsui Busan Kaisha of Japan and Amtorg Trading Company of Russia. Fokker Aircraft of Holland assembled and marketed the DC-3s in Europe. Manufacturers in Japan produced 487 of the DC-3s, and the Russians rolled out 2,000 to 3,000 of the aircraft from their assembly lines.

With the onset of World War II, many of the commercial DC-3s operated by airlines were put into military service. Additional assembly lines were added to existing Douglas plants to produce the military cargo versions of the DC-3, the C-47.

With beefed-up landing gear, a double cargo door, floor tie-downs, and folding bench seats, the C-47s started to roll into service for the Army, Navy, and Allies at an amazing rate. At its peak, production reached 573 planes per month or 18.5 planes a day.

Pilots, navigators, cargo crews, and ground crews all attested to the durability and rugged dependability of the C-47s. With its principal role being the transporting of troops and the delivering of supplies and munitions, the plane justly deserved its reputation as the "workhorse of the air." Many of the men who flew the craft maintain that the C-47s were the most forgiving, reliable, useful, and best planes ever flown.

Today DC-3 associations say that 1,500 to 2,000 DC-3s are still in operation throughout the world. Early this year an estimated 500 aircraft were still in military use for various nations. Douglas Aircraft officials also estimate that another 1,100 DC-3s can be found in air museums and in use by sky-diving schools, collectors, and other private operators.

The durable DC-3 marks a half-century of flight.

World Trade Center Opens

(1988, December) The Greater Los Angeles World Trade Center has opened its doors. Among the first tenants occupying the impressive structure are the accounting firms Peat, Marwick, Mitchell and Company; Ernst and Whinney; and DeLoitte, Haskins and Sells. The brokerage house of Bateman, Eichler, Hill, Richards is also an early tenant in the center.

Currently 70 percent of the Phase I tower is leased. The total construction

The new, 27-story World Trade Center is the tallest building in the San Pedro Bay area.

plan calls for a four-phase build-out. Phase II is the development of a world-class hotel on the southwest corner of the center. Phases III and IV are in the planning stages and will consist of additional towers. Total square footage of the center will be 2.2 million. The first phase tower offers 428,000 square feet of office and retail space.

Sponsored by the Port of Long Beach, which acquired the 12.7-acre site in downtown Long Beach, the international business center is a joint venture of Long Beach-based IDM Corporation and Kajima International, Inc., Japan's largest construction firm. The glass-and-marble structure rises 27 stories above Ocean Boulevard and is certain to be a new landmark on the shores of San Pedro Bay. A later tower will stand even taller at 35 stories.

Located on the eastern edge of the Pacific Rim, the Trade Center will serve the world trade community of all Southern California. Overlooking America's leading harbor complex of Los Angeles/Long Beach, the Center will service international businesses of all types and sizes.

In addition to the hotel, a World Trade Center Association will offer research, telecommunications, and educational services to the world trader. And the World Trade Club will offer its members a convenient setting to meet and entertain guests and clients.

A review of potential operators of the hotel is currently being conducted and an announcement is expected in the spring of next year. Phase II construction of the hotel will commence in 1990.

San Pedro Bay—Nation's Leading Port Complex

(1988) Confirming what had been expected for several years, the San Pedro Bay, comprised of the ports of Long Beach and Los Angeles, is now officially the leading seaport of America.

Trade experts had predicted for several years that the Southern California harbor complex, already handling 60 percent of all cargo entering the U.S. West Coast, would soon dethrone New York/New Jersey as the nation's most important maritime center of trade and commerce.

U.S. Customs figures show that Long Beach/Los Angeles recorded revenue collections of $2.5 billion compared to New York/New Jersey's $1.8 billion. Vessels numbering 7,106 called at San Pedro Bay versus 5,579 at the previous East Coast leader. Long Beach moved a record 68.7 million tons of cargo across its berths in the past year. Los Angeles, sharing the San Pedro Bay, recorded its best year in cargo tonnage with 66.3 million tons of products loaded and off-loaded.

In the highly lucrative and competitive container cargo field, Long Beach/Los Angeles combined for a total of 2.9 million TEUs (20-foot equivalent units) of containers moved across the berths of the twin Southern California giants. (A 20-foot equivalent unit is the unit of measurement that equals a 20-foot ocean cargo container.)

Individually, Los Angeles and Long Beach rank 9th and 11th, respectively, in comparison to other container ports worldwide.

The boom in U.S.-Asia trade that began to mushroom in the late 1970s found the ports of San Pedro Bay in a fortuitous confluence of timing and location. With trade with Japan and other Pacific Rim nations accelerating, West Coast ports were especially situated to capitalize on this boom. Further, with 12 million consumers in the immediate area, international shippers were more than compelled to utilize Los Angeles and Long Beach.

The lead that San Pedro Bay has taken over other American seaports will be certain to increase as trans-Pacific trade continues to outperform trans-Atlantic commerce. This, combined with the fact that the world's most dynamic growth economies are located in the Far East and Southeast Asia, appears to assure that the San Pedro Bay will maintain its role as America's most important international maritime trade complex.

The Port of Long Beach

Top: San Pedro Bay is the nation's leading port complex. Bottom: The Port of Los Angeles

Todd Delivers Last Ship

(1989, June) The frigate *Ingraham* was delivered to the U.S. Navy today, sliding down the ways in the drydock and splashing into the waters of San Pedro. The event was accompanied with the usual fanfare and speeches from politicians and company officials. People cheered; flags were waved; and workers beamed with pride over a job well done.

And then, an hour later, Todd Shipyard executives announced that the yard that has been an institution in the harbor for generations and has provided ships for the Navy for two world wars, a police action, and an ambivalent conflict in Southeast Asia, would shutter its docks in three months.

The *Ingraham* was the last of 18 frigates that the yard delivered to the Navy on a $3-billion contract. During the height of production, 5,600 workers streamed throughout the yard at all hours of the day. With no new contracts in the offing, Todd is expected to start slashing jobs in anticipation of the long-dreaded closure.

Todd had long sought to obtain work for its San Pedro yard, but none was forthcoming. High labor costs and foreign competition finally wrought their damage on the yard. Two years ago, parent company, Todd Shipyards of New Jersey, filed for protection under Chapter 11 of the federal bankruptcy laws. Last year the San Pedro plant reported losses of $84.9 million; two years ago that figure stood at $28.1 million.

For the last seven years, union members agreed to a wage freeze that may have prolonged the life of the yard but also bred animosity directed at management and its operating policies.

A retired Navy rear admiral who monitored Todd's contracts said that it was his belief that the company directed work to its Seattle yard because of the lower wages at that yard. Workers there are paid $1.50 an hour less than the San Pedro shipyard's employees.

Union officials pointed accusatory fingers at management's perceived questionable procedures and cronyism. Management pointed their fingers at the spiraling wages that Todd's employees received. And, fingers also were directed at the Los Angeles Harbor Department and its lease with the yard, a lease that required a monthly payment of $225,000 for the 112 acres of Harbor Department land.

The shipyard began its life as the Los Angeles Shipbuilding and Drydock Corporation in 1917, when it built wooden cargo vessels and steel-hulled Navy combat ships during World War I.

In the Second World War, Todd took over the company when it encountered difficulty in meeting its

Todd's last ship slides down the ways.

commitment to deliver Liberty and Victory ships to the Federal Maritime Commission. Todd produced more than 6 million tons of new ships during this period.

Todd will continue to operate two other shipyards after the San Pedro facility closes in September. Besides the Seattle yard, a shipyard in Galveston, Texas, will still remain open.

Todd's huge San Pedro shipyard.

Camp Drum to Support Union Cause

Signal Hill Gusher Springs to Life

Longshoreman Killed in Strike Melee

Killer Quake Hits Long Beach

Pedro Shipyd Humm

Gambling Ship Commodore Cashes in Chips

"YANKEE DONS BUY RANCHOS

Navy Shipyard To Be Built

Long B Selecte Headqu

San Pedro Bay— Nation's Leading Port Complex

Tanker Blast Kills Five

Vincent Thomas Bridge Opens

SENATOR WINS PORT FOR

A "Queen" Arrives in Long Beach

Chapter 7

Chronicles of Enterprise

1896-1989

The San Pedro Bay area's past and present are a harmonious blend of seafaring legends, multicultural life-styles, and modern-day business vitality.

Many area businesses date from the days of schooners and square riggers. Their founders were waterfront pioneers with a vision for developing the natural harbor from sand flat to the long crescent wharf of the late 1800s. Now these enterprising descendants and present-day pioneers are steering San Pedro Bay area business into the fast-flowing current of the 1990s with as much verve and expectation as their ancestors.

While the rope slings and handcarts that moved goods across wooden docks have yielded to containerized shipping and remarkable high-speed technologies, the waterfront flavor—the ever-present lure of the sea—still pervades the community.

Rudolph Valentino and Zane Grey do not roam the waterfront these days, but many less-famous sailors do make local marinas home base. Foreign sailors needing medical treatment do not go to a little red-brick hospital, but rather a big one with multilingual capabilities in 22 languages.

San Pedro Bay area businesses have added to their colorful histories while contributing heartily to the growth of their community. The organizations whose stories appear on the following pages have chosen to participate in this literary project. Many San Pedro businesses served the nation's war efforts when needed and fueled its peace effort through trade that reaches around the globe many times while moving toward the twenty-first century.

San Pedro Bay Area Enterprise 1896-1989

1896 Joseph Fellows, Sr., influential in founding the pleasure-boat industry in Southern California, opens his first shipyard.

1899 A group of local businessmen creates the Crescent Wharf and Warehouse Co. to improve business in San Pedro Bay.

1903 Al Larson leases land from the Banning family to start his waterfront boat shop.

1907 Los Angeles City Charter creates a board of harbor commissioners.

1911 The Port of Long Beach officially opens.

1919 Romolo and John Rados open the Harbor Boat Building Company.

1923 Metropolitan Stevedore Company is founded with a staff of seven.

1924 Doctors and local businessmen organize and incorporate the San Pedro General Hospital Association.

1925 The San Pedro General Hospital Association dedicates its first building.

1928 Crescent Wharf and Warehouse Co. acquires the stevedoring interests of Spreckles Co.

1931 The Harbor Department takes over control of Long Beach harbor.

1932 Joe Fellows Yacht and Launch Co. adds marina operations to its business.

1937 The San Pedro General Hospital Association is reorganized under the new name of San Pedro Hospital.

1939 E.A. Hackett and Maurice Buckhands purchase the Los Angeles division of the California Cotton Mills, rename it the California Cotton Fumigating Company, and establish Wilmington as its home base.

1942-1944 The Fellows Yacht and Launch Co. builds and repairs vessels for the Navy and Army Transportation Corps.

1948 The San Pedro Hospital Association converts from a private stock corporation to a nonprofit community hospital known as San Pedro Community Hospital•Dr. William R. Anderson sets up his clinic on West Sixth Street in San Pedro•Green Hills Memorial Park is dedicated.

1951 The first permanent building in Green Hills Memorial Park is dedicated.

1956 Crescent Wharf and Warehouse Co. purchases the Outer Harbor Dock and Wharf Co. in the Port of Los Angeles.

1957 Green Hills Memorial Park becomes a nonprofit corporation.

1959 Andrew Wall buys the Al Larson Boat Shop, the oldest privately operated shipyard in the Los Angeles area then (and now).

1961 San Pedro Community Hospital (now named San Pedro Peninsula Hospital) dedicates a new, five-story building.

1962 Hugo Neu-Proler Co. is founded as a joint venture between Hugo Neu & Sons, Inc. and Proler International Corp.•The Prolerizer, which can shred automobiles, is first installed at Hugo Neu-Proler Co.•Hugo Neu-Proler revolutionizes ship loading by designing and constructing the first apron-mounted steel belt conveyor for bulk loading all grades of scrap metal into awaiting vessels.

1963 The Vincent Thomas Bridge links WORLDPORT LA, the interstate freeway system, and the Port of Long Beach.

1965 The California Cotton Fumigating Company moves into Berth 155-A, where it has remained ever since.

1967 Fellows and Stewart Company, formerly Joe Fellows Yacht and Launch Co., sells its shipyard and becomes mostly a marina business.

1968 Crescent Wharf and Warehouse Co. purchases Jones Stevedoring Company•Chang Yung-Fa launches Evergreen Marine Corp., an international shipping business.

1975 The Harbor Boat Building Company closes down•Evergreen Marine Corp. launches service from Taiwan to the U.S. Atlantic Coast.

1977 Evergreen Marine Corp. begins service from Taiwan to the West Coast•Art Engel establishes Southwest Marine, Inc.

1979 Expansion of San Pedro Peninsula Hospital is completed•The Los Angeles Maritime Museum opens its doors at Berth 84 in San Pedro.

1980 The Wall family constructs the Oyster Wharf restaurant in San Pedro and opens the San Pedro Marina on the main channel in Los Angeles Harbor•Terry J. Coniglio opens his law practice and begins serving shipping industry clients.

1981 Long Beach's Foreign Trade Zone No. 50 opens•Southwest Marine, Inc. acquires the former Bethlehem Steel shipyard in Los Angeles Harbor.

1983 Stevedoring Services of America is formed after Seattle Stevedore purchases Crescent Wharf and Warehouse Company and Brady-Hamilton Stevedore Company•The Los Angeles Maritime Museum becomes part of the Department of Parks and Recreation of the City of Los Angeles.

1984 Evergreen Marine Corp. initiates two-way, around-the-world, regular weekly full-container service.

1985 Dr. Anthony Rippo purchases Anderson Medical Group•Evergreen Marine Corp. inaugurates service from the Far East to the Red Sea and East Mediterranean.

1986 Evergreen Marine Corp. introduces its first double-stack train service in the U.S.

1988 Phase I of the Port of Long Beach-sponsored Greater Los Angeles World Trade Center opens.

1989 Metropolitan Stevedore Company opens new headquarters•Anderson Medical Group merges with Bay Harbor Hospital•Southwest Marine, Inc., acquires Northwest Marine Iron Works.

Fellows & Stewart Company

Founded 1896
Joseph Fellows, Sr., Founder, 1896-1942
Victor B. Stewart, 1910-1946
Joseph Fellows, Jr., 1929-1961
Lois M. Fellows, 1961-1967
Richard J. Fellows, 1962-present

PLEASURE-CRAFT PIONEER

FIRST-CLASS CUSTOM BOATS

(1896-1930) As the first shipbuilder in the area and one of the first shipyards on Terminal Island, Joe Fellows Yacht and Launch Co. was a widely known business that built custom boats and yachts of any size—both sail and motor powered.

Joseph Fellows, Sr., who established what was to become a three-generational family business, was influential in founding the pleasure-boat industry in Southern California.

Born in England, he immigrated first to Canada, then to Minnesota and Seattle, where he lived on a boat until he moved to San Francisco to start building them. He was drawn to Southern California in its halcyon days to open his first yard in 1896.

By 1910 Fellows had taken a partner, Victor B. Stewart, but kept the name of the business and its specialty the same for a number of years. He

Fellows & Stewart built this 110-foot sub chaser in 1942 for the U.S. Navy.

supplied motion-picture and business tycoons with pleasure craft and earned the reputation as the man to see to buy a boat. Rudolph Valentino bought a 32 footer and novelist Zane Grey commissioned several boats, as did producer Hal Roach.

Fellows was a charter member of every major yacht club in the area and was both a sailor and power-boat racer. His son, Joe Fellows, Jr., joined him in the company in 1929.

HELPING WARTIME NEEDS

(1930-1950) The yacht business continued strong through the 1930s, with marina operations added in 1932. At one time there were 450 slips, the largest marina under one ownership in the area.

But yacht production was suspended in 1942 for four years while the firm helped with the war effort. During World War II Fellows handled building and repair work for U.S. Navy and Army Transportation Corps vessels and at one point was bulging at the seams with about 400 employees. In 1944, a proud moment for the Fellows family, a Merchant Marine liberty ship was named for Joseph Fellows, Sr. Two years later his son—a naval architect, marine engineer, and distinguished sailor—took over as company president.

SECOND-GENERATION OWNER

(1950-present) Within four years there were major changes in the company. Commercial work—fishing boats and military craft—filled the yard. Under Joe Jr.'s tenure, the firm

A 47-foot island clipper, built in 1947.

built two steel crew boats for ARAMCO for use in the Persian Gulf.

Fellows & Stewart Company sold the shipyard in 1967, when Richard Fellows took over the helm, and the firm became mostly a marina business. Today, with his wife, Lois, Fellows oversees R&L Fellows Company at Berth 99 on Terminal Island and also manufactures floating dock systems for saltwater marinas. Richard, as general engineering contractor, proudly carries on his family's maritime heritage, but would rather "build ships than sail them" as his legacy to the sea.

Stevedoring Services of America

Founded 1899
F.D. "Ricky" Smith, President
David L. Michou, Regional Vice President

GROWTH REFLECTS STRONG ROOTS

Terminal Island in the early 1900s provided a barren backdrop for the fledgling Crescent Wharf and Warehouse Co., a predecessor company of Stevedoring Services of America. Crescent took its name from the long, curving wharf that welcomed early lumber schooners to port.

COMPANY PRECEDES TWO PORTS

(1899-1928) Even before the local breakwater was built or the ports were formally organized, Stevedoring Services of America was on the scene under the name Crescent Wharf and Warehouse Co. The operation was created by a group of local businessmen who saw the need for improving trade in San Pedro Bay.

Crescent started out modestly, handling lumber shipments coming into the rapidly growing area, but soon grew to handling goods brought by sailing ships that braved the notorious Cape Horn.

The company developed with San Pedro Bay. When the remarkable growth in San Francisco shipping began to trickle south, dockhands and shippers alike were convinced of the potential for expanding the southern port.

Crescent took its name from the shape of the long, curving wharf on the Terminal Island side of the harbor, and the firm focused on stevedoring and warehousing.

CRESCENT EXPANDS

(1928-1959) Serving a growing roster of shippers, trading companies, port authorities, steamship operators, and consignees in the Los Angeles/Long Beach area was not enough for Crescent. In 1928 the firm acquired the stevedoring interests of Spreckles Co. and extended to the Port of San Diego. The port was growing rapidly and gave Crescent the opportunity to enter into terminal operation, ships' husbandry, and bonded warehousing to provide more complete service.

By 1956 Crescent was ready to purchase the Outer Harbor Dock and Wharf Co. in the Port of Los Angeles, formerly owned by Southern Pacific Railway and Union Oil Company. This added substantially to its inventory of terminals, equipment, and staff.

And, in 1968, Crescent made a bold move when it purchased Jones Stevedoring Company, going into the San Francisco Bay Area market for the first time.

SEATTLE STEVEDORE COMPANY

(1959-1968) While Crescent was expanding in the south, another firm called Seattle Stevedore Company was on the move also. Founded in 1918, the firm was acquired in 1954 by Fred Smith and A.S. Coe. In 1958, upon Coe's death, Melvin Stewart joined the firm as partner to Fred Smith, and this management team carried the company into an era of expansion and innovation.

When containerization revolutionized the industry in the 1950s and 1960s, Seattle Stevedore began the practice of maintaining and repairing containers and chassis in hours through Container Equipment Maintenance (CEM), an endeavor that earned the firm the reputation as a pioneer. CEM work means every unit is returned with 100 percent usability and minimum downtime, as the maintenance staff services, repairs, and tests every kind of container, chassis, and related equipment in use.

Innovative in the 1960s, when cargo handling moved from sling and hook toward palletized operations, Seattle Stevedore introduced pneumatic trucks to docks in volume. In 1964 the firm used floating cranes for conventional log loading, then worked with several trading companies to produce the first log export yards in Pacific

Northwest ports. In 1966 the firm pioneered other notable cargo-handling equipment. By the 1970s Seattle Stevedore was serving all ports in Puget Sound and along Washington's Pacific coast.

SUCCESSORS TAKE CHARGE

(1970-1988) In the early 1970s Fred Smith and Mel Stewart passed control and ownership of the business to their sons, Ricky Smith and Tom Stewart. Under this new leadership the company saw phenomenal growth and diversification take place, including a joint venture between Seattle Stevedore and Crescent. As the container revolution grew, the new team established new terminals, operations, and a larger presence on the West Coast.

In 1983 Stevedoring Services of America was formed after Seattle Stevedore had purchased Crescent Wharf and Warehouse Company in California and Brady-Hamilton Stevedore Company in Oregon, and established close affiliations with

Southeast Stevedoring Corp. in Alaska. Each company brought rich histories, substantial reputations, extensive resources, and recognized expertise to the merger. Now, as the largest stevedore and terminal contractor on the West Coast, SSA launched a new corporate culture, blending decades of professionalism and high standards to serve the commerce, trade, and transportation industries all along the U.S. West Coast.

NEW OWNERSHIP, SAME FOCUS

(1989-present) In April 1989 SSA became a wholly owned company under the Smith family. Ricky Smith is president, working with an executive committee. Included in the new team are senior vice presidents Dan Flynn, marketing; Claude Stritmatter, outports; Ed DeNike, operations; Jon Hemingway, administration/finance; regional vice president Dave Michou, Southern California; and vice president Dan Phaneuf, contracts/billing.

Today's SSA performs services and provides facilities at all ports along the U.S. West Coast.

All year long and at any time of day, dockworkers load and discharge, receive and deliver, move and warehouse thousands of tons of import and export cargo of every type imaginable: automobiles, fresh fruit, bagged

Pacific Container Terminal at the Port of Long Beach handles more than 100,000 containers per year. In the background is Pier F, SSA's terminal for steel and other break-bulk cargoes.

An overview of the Indies Terminal shows an outstanding facility at which up to six ships can dock to unload a variety of goods and commodities, from autos to fruit, newsprint to containers.

goods, cotton bales, sophisticated electronics, raw logs, bulk commodities, and more.

All stevedoring methods are employed, including rail-ramp operations and directly loading/off-loading trains. All types of vessels can be handled: from automobile carriers to passenger liners, from container vessels to bulk ships.

The company has an ongoing and solid working relationship with the International Longshoremen's and

Warehousemen's Union, which has worked closely with SSA on safety matters and technology advances. This alliance has helped shippers, carriers, and the ports succeed and advance toward the future with confidence.

Stevedoring Services of America is headquartered in Seattle, with regional offices in Long Beach (at the end of Pier F); Portland, Oregon; and Oakland, California. Its motto, familiar to customers along its route, is, "From Alaska to California, we've got you covered."

Al Larson Boat Shop

Established 1903
Al Larson, Founder
Gloria Wall, President

IN COMMUNITY FOUR GENERATIONS

Large private yacht in dry dock for repairs.

WATERFRONT PIONEERS
(1903-1918) The Wall family and the Al Larson Boat Shop officially got together in 1959, but both the family and the shop brought long maritime histories to the merger.

Al Larson, a Swede who came to Los Angeles in the early 1900s, leased some land from the famous Banning family to start his waterfront boat shop in 1903. Meanwhile, there were two families in the area who were establishing their presence with ethnic diversity and love of the sea and who would later join the Larson family.

In 1894 a Danish sea captain named Reynold Wall came to San Pedro in search of his older brother. Wall, who had been in the British Merchant Marine, learned through a seaman's union in San Francisco that his brother might be in the San Pedro area. He soon found him and then decided to stay there.

Wall got his master's license in 1913 and took a job as master of the Banning family yacht. Later he joined the Los Angeles Harbor Department as a tug operator, then a port pilot.

TWO FAMILIES BUILD BASE
(1919-1958) In 1919 another family was getting established in San Pedro. Romolo Rados and his son John, recent immigrants from what is now Yugoslavia, brought their boat-building prowess to the area and opened the Harbor Boat Building Company. By the time World War II started, the firm had already designed and built 17 yachts, 32 fishing vessels, and 20 U.S. Navy ships. As the city grew and prospered, so did the Rados business.

Meanwhile, Wall and his wife, Louise, had two sons, George and Andrew. George chose medicine as a career, while Andrew went to sea as a cadet on several merchant marine ships. He passed his ensign's exam for the Coast Guard Reserve and in 1942 entered active duty, earned his aviator's wings the following year, and was a pilot until the end of World War II.

At this point the families intermingled. Andrew married Gloria Rados, daughter of the man who helped start Harbor Boat Building Company, and went to work for his father-in-law.

CHANGING OF THE GUARD
(1959-1980) Andrew Wall purchased the Al Larson Boat Shop in 1959, starting his own establishment with five employees and a business that was one-sixth the size it is today. Along with the business he purchased the Larson traditions—a top reputation and community recognition. Then, as now, it was the oldest privately operated shipyard in the Los Angeles area.

Odd stories from the early days abound, including one about a chronically leaky boat brought to the shop for repairs. When it was hauled out of the water, workers found a simple reason: a swordfish beak stuck into its side.

In the mid-1960s the shop took a step toward servicing pleasure craft, building the Al Larson Marina in the Port of Los Angeles. The 125-slip facility handles craft of 20 to 50 feet.

The Harbor Boat Building Company remained intact until the 1960s, when it became part of LTV Corporation. Subseqently it went through several other transfers of ownership, but always with a member of the Rados family at the helm. In 1968 John Rados died, and seven years later the business finally closed its doors after nearly 50 years of operation.

REPAIRS, RESTAURANTS, AND MARINAS (1980-1984)

In 1980 the Wall family diversified its business with construction of the Oyster Wharf restaurant in San Pedro in the Ports of Call Village, and at the same time it opened a 100-slip marina on the main channel in Los Angeles Harbor called San Pedro Marina.

When Andrew died in 1984, the boat shop was at a major turning point. His wife, Gloria, then secretary/treasurer, became president. With sons Jack Wall and George Wall as vice presidents, representing the fourth generation in the maritime family, Gloria bought additional land in Long Beach and expanded their commercial business.

TECHNOLOGY BLENDS WITH TRADITION (1985-present)

Conversions and repair of mid-size vessels constitute most of the shop's work. Among its many projects are the Long Beach fireboat fleet repair, the conversion of supply vessels to firefighting vessels for offshore oil drilling, U.S. Navy frigates and battleships, Coast Guard vessels, local barges and tugs, fishing fleets, and private vessels.

The shipyard is a completely self-contained operation with fully equipped machine, carpenter, welding, paint, electrical, and pipe-fitting shops.

Al Larson Boat Shop considers itself a small yard, with some 150 employees in boat yard operations at 1046 Seaside Avenue, Terminal Island. The company's adjacent Larson Marina and its San Pedro Marina with Oyster Wharf restaurant bring the total to about 220. A good many employees have long tenures with the company, adding to Al Larson Boat Shop's stature as the patriarch of the area's boat-repair industry.

The marinas currently maintain about the same number of slips, 100 in San Pedro (a most impressive location because of the marina's proximity to ship traffic in the Port of Los Angeles) and 130 at the Larson Marina. Many of

Welding and all other types of marine repairs are performed at Al Larson Boat Shop.

Removal of propellor shafting from local harbor tug.

the slips have been held by the same lessee for years. This type of longevity has created good relations with customers in the harbor and made the boat shop more of a neighbor than a place of business, according to management.

Even though the Walls intend to keep Al Larson Boat Shop small to mid-size, soon it will need an enlarged facility to handle even the best controlled growth. And a fifth generation of the Rados/Wall family is poised to continue its distinguished heritage in maritime service to San Pedro.

WORLDPORT LA

Established 1907
Jun Mori, Esq., President, Los Angeles Board of Harbor
Commissioners
Dr. E. Grace Payne, Vice President
Robert Rados, Sr., Commissioner
Floyd Clay, Commissioner
Ronald S. Lushing, Commissioner
Ezunial Burts, Executive Director

WORLD-CLASS PORT

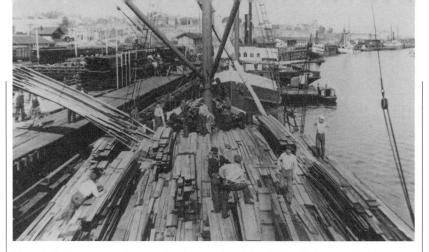

The principal cargo moved across the wharves of early San Pedro Harbor was lumber, needed to sustain the building boom of turn-of-the-century Los Angeles.

UP FROM THE MUD FLATS
(1907-1963) The Port of Los Angeles got its official start when a governing board of harbor commissioners was created by Los Angeles City Charter in 1907, though the area had been developing since the late 1800s when it was little more than a mud flat. Terminal Island, once called Rattlesnake Island, was transformed over the years from a narrow uninhabited sandbar to a military and commercial shipping hub.

BRIDGING THE GAP
(1963-1989) It was not until 1963, when the Vincent Thomas Bridge—then dubbed the Bridge to Nowhere—was built, that a link was fused between WORLDPORT LA, the growing inter-

state freeway system, and the Port of Long Beach. Both ports gained stature in the 1960s through container shipping and surged again in the early 1980s through Pacific Rim trade.

By 1989 WORLDPORT LA's total foreign trade was valued at $45 billion. Total cargo handled from approximately 4,000 vessels reached 66.3 million metric revenue tons and led to a gross revenue of $150 million in 1989.

Not only a leading cargo port handling a record 2.1 million cargo containers, WORLDPORT LA is also a major passenger port. More than a half-million passengers used the World Cruise Center in 1989. New passengership facilities and the formation of an efficient consortium of

cruise lines has made Los Angeles the number-one passenger port on the West Coast.

COMMERCE AND RECREATION THRIVE
(1989-present) WORLDPORT LA is a $760-million facility encompassing 7,500 acres of land and sheltered water, with 28 miles of improved waterfront. A landlord port with 800 employees, it provides shippers with a wide variety of cargo terminals and facilities. Eight spacious container terminals offer more than 500 acres of container handling and back land—all within four miles of the Intermodal Container Transfer Facility, the West Coast's largest, most automated container transfer facilty for truck-to-rail movements.

Recreational facilities include some 6,500 boat slips, dozens of international restaurants, fine beaches, and sportfishing.

WORLDPORT LA has

invested in the future, along with its neighboring Port of Long Beach, in the 2020 Program, which will nearly double port land and facilities to keep pace with world trade trends in the next three decades. As a phased program of dredging, landfilling, and facilities construction, the plan is a carefully designed blueprint that provides the basis for the largest integrated marine/ highway/rail transportation hub in the world.

The $760-million, 7,500-acre WORLDPORT LA offers shippers 28 miles of improved waterfront and the outstanding facilities of the West Coast's leading commercial harbor.

Port of Long Beach

Established 1911

Steven R. Dillenbeck, Acting Executive Director and
Managing Director/Commerce and Development Bureau
Paul E. Brown, Managing Director/Administration and
Maintenance Bureau
Leland R. Hill, Managing Director/Planning and
Engineering Bureau

GROWTH THROUGH PROGRESSIVE VISION

OPENING THE PORT

(1911-1965) The Port of Long Beach officially opened in 1911, with the dedication of its first wharf. Although a natural harbor, first visited by Juan Rodriguez Cabrillo in 1542, the port area needed extensive development to make it useable for maritime trade and commerce. Through the efforts of a few enterprising businesspeople, the inner harbor area was opened to the sea by dredging through a large sandbar and later protected by a long breakwater. The ocean entrance was completed in 1909, the same year voters approved a $245,000 bond issue for water frontage on which to build a pier.

Growth during the next two decades was slow but steady for the City of Long Beach-owned port. In 1931 the harbor was placed under the control of the Harbor Department, which established itself as a landlord, leasing or assigning docks, wharves, transit sheds, and terminals to private firms. Discovery of oil on Harbor District land that same year provided funds for port development for the next 34 years until the mid-1960s, when oil revenues were transferred to the City of Long Beach and the State of California.

TRADE CENTER ESTABLISHED

(1965-1984) Since 1965 Port of Long Beach expansion has been funded solely by harbor-generated revenues—thanks largely to the advent of containerization of cargo. The port has grown to 11.9 square miles, with 4.7 square miles of land, 12 piers, and 70 operational cargo berths, all located within two miles of open sea.

In the 1980s, as cargo movement shifted dramatically from the Atlantic Ocean to the Pacific, Long Beach captured a leading position among West Coast ports. It has been the tonnage leader for the past 10 years.

Another major event for the port was the opening in 1981 of the Long Beach Foreign Trade Zone No. 50, the only such facility in the region. Offering duty-free manufacturing, assembly, distribution, and warehousing facilities, FTZ No. 50 has quickly gained stature, reflecting the unlimited growth potential of the region.

FUTURISTIC PROJECTS

(1985-present) In early 1985 Long Beach joined with the Port of Los Angeles and the Southern Pacific Transportation Company to enhance the intermodal facilities of both harbors. The result of this joint effort is the Intermodal Container Transfer Facility (ICTF), located four miles from the docks.

The Port of Long Beach-sponsored Greater Los Angeles World Trade Center in downtown Long Beach is a significant international venture by IDM Corporation and Kajima International of Japan. Phase I opened in 1988, and, when the complex is completed, it will offer 2.2 million square feet of prime space for office, exhibit, meeting, and related trade activities.

Further joint development of San Pedro Bay is couched in the 2020 Program, which will add four square miles to both ports by the year 2020 at a cost of $4 billion.

The Port of Long Beach is expanding its Pier J container facilities by 147 acres of new land being added seaward from existing terminals. Additional container berths are also under construction on the Seventh Street peninsula.

Metropolitan Stevedore Company

Founded 1923

Chester Eschen, Jr., Chairman of the Board
Brian Y. Harrison, President and Chief Executive Officer
Henry R. Ottenstroer, Senior Vice President
Edward J. Kaveney, Chief Financial Officer
Robert P. Senecal, Vice President/Bulk Operations
Robert B. Roach, Vice President/Equipment and
  Maintenance
James R. Callahan, Vice President/Insurance
Robert T. Chiu, Assistant Vice President

PACESETTER IN ITS INDUSTRY

NINETEENTH-CENTURY ROOTS
(1852-1950) Metropolitan Stevedore Company has solid and colorful roots. It sprung from the parent California Stevedore and Ballast Company, established by two Danish sea captains, Eschen and Minor, in San Francisco in 1852. The founders' successors spun off Metropolitan in 1923 as a wholly owned subsidiary because they believed that Los Angeles had potential.

The company used what was sophisticated equipment at the time—rope slings and handcarts—to service the wooden docks, giving the fledgling Metropolitan Stevedore Company an early reputation for offering clientele in the Los Angeles/Long Beach harbor area the very latest in heavy-lift handling. In those days a stevedore, someone who loads and unloads ships, was known as "the man with the hook," which was used to move crates, boxes, and bales around the dock. Early cargoes, though small by today's standards, consisted of familiar items: exotic fruits, seafood, ore, and general goods.

CONTAINERS CHANGE THE INDUSTRY
(1950-1970) Container shipping, quite simply, revolutionized the industry in the 1950s. The metal boxes, resembling truck-trailers and equipped with special corner fittings for movement and storage, could hold any kind of cargo. More than that, they could go directly from the factory to the warehouse, minimizing handling, breakage, and pilfering.

In addition, the containers meshed well with advancing computer technology for increased productivity, greater cost control, and better service. The huge metal containers, stacked on special square-sterned vessels, could be directed by electronic manifests and routed around the globe with ease. By the 1970s Metropolitan was handling nearly 6 million tons of cargo each year.

Coastal environment protection has been high on Metropolitan's priority list for decades. For example, when Pier G opened in 1962 for dry-bulk handling, Metropolitan, as ongoing operator, set up three large dust-collection units with a combined air-filtration capacity of 167,000 cubic feet per minute, which effectively sealed the facilities against the escape of airborne particles. Metropolitan was instrumental both in the design and modification of the bulk terminal, which, as one of the largest and most sophisticated of its type in the nation, includes seven miles

Original bulkloader operated by Metropolitan in the early 1930s.

Working a general cargo vessel with a steam-driven crane in the early days.

of a completely automated ship-to-dock conveyor system.

At the same pier, settling tanks were added to maintain water quality at the facility. The tanks are designed to trap any surface or rain runoff water from flowing directly into the ocean. Only after the water is sufficiently treated is it allowed to be discharged, thus preventing possible contamination.

RIDING A NEW WAVE
(1970-1988) As recently as 20 years ago, a ship stayed in port for several weeks to have its holds emptied. But containers and technology have condensed the process to a single eight-hour stevedore shift.

Metropolitan's work with auto imports has changed drastically over the years as well. Gone are the days when each vehicle was lifted over the vessel's side in a conventional sling. Now stevedores board the specialized auto carriers that look like floating parking garages, carrying up to 4,500 cars, and drive the vehicles down customized, built-in ramps.

Metropolitan's cargo list has grown over the past two decades to include virtually everything except petroleum, but including petroleum by-products. On the list are coal/potash, liquid chemicals, bananas, container cargo, cars, steel, and even foodstuffs, baggage, and passengers for various cruise ships. Metropolitan uses its specially designed and patented lift cage to load delicate fresh fruits outbound for international markets.

Contemporary issues—as well as technologies—demand Metropolitan's attention as an industry leader. Metropolitan has scored significant achievements in employee safety and environmental concerns, receiving several safety awards from the Pacific Maritime Association. It was the first Southern California company to receive top honors in the coastwide class A stevedore safety division.

METROPOLITAN'S MISSION
(present) Almost 70 years later Metropolitan is still known as an innovator in the ever-advancing maritime industry. As a full-service general contractor and one of Southern California's largest cargo-handling businesses, the company also operates various terminal facilities in the two intermodal ports.

No longer a subsidiary but its own entity, Metropolitan is chaired by founder Captain Eschen's grandson. The firm has grown from an original staff of seven in 1923 to more than 140 salaried positions and some 300 union personnel on a standby basis to handle its high-volume business. Now both men and women work with sophisticated high-technology equipment to handle bulk commodities and containers.

Located in Wilmington since 1923 and on the same spot since 1948, the company built and opened new headquarters in 1989 at 720 East E Street. The handsome, modern 65,000-square-foot structure will accommodate Metropolitan's increased emphasis on a high-technology-oriented, twenty-first-century expansion.

As a service organization, Metropolitan Stevedore Company relies on its long history of professionalism to serve both large and small shippers. Company officials emphasize efficiency, adaptation, innovation, sense of community, and high commitment to quality service among their objectives for continued excellence.

San Pedro Peninsula Hospital

Founded 1925
John M. Wilson, President
Gene Iker, Vice President/Medical Support Services
Barbara Skala, Vice President/Patient Care Services
R. Don Olden, Vice President/Finance

LOOKING AHEAD FOR YOUR SAKE

THE BEGINNING

(1925-1927) Things change. In the 65 years San Pedro Peninsula Hospital has been serving the community, it has seen its pediatric patients become adult patients and seen its adults become members of the Senior Preference program.

The hospital has come a long way from the modest brick building that was dedicated on June 14, 1925, by the Reverend Martin Luther Thomas. It had been organized the prior year by a group of doctors and local businessmen and incorporated as the San Pedro General Hospital Association.

The hospital was built at a cost of $19,000 on its original site at 1305 West Sixth Street. Fred W. Reynolds, M.D., served as the association's first president, and Mary Jane Currie, R.N., was the hospital's first administrator. There were four registered nurses on staff at the time. The single-story, multiple-wing format had 19 beds, a major operating room, a minor surgery room for emergencies, and a delivery room.

Only two months after it opened, the hospital had an average daily bed census of 29. Expansion two years later added a $40,000 two-story center wing that raised the bed capacity to 57 and included a nurses' home as well as radiology and laboratory capabilities.

SPACE AND SERVICES INCREASE

(1928-1937) As the community grew, the hospital added space and services, with an obstetrical wing in 1928, and a staff that had grown to 44 employees—including 23 nurses. No further additions were made until 1938, when the surgical rooms were enlarged and modernized and a new kitchen was built.

To avoid confusion with the county hospital, San Pedro General Hospital was reorganized in 1937 under the new name of San Pedro Hospital.

EXPANSION CONTINUES

(1938-1947) Growth became the norm for San Pedro Hospital, with continued construction to meet the community's needs. By 1943 a typical daily patient census was 113 adults and 30 babies (though official capacity was 107 beds and 18 bassinets). The new west wing was built in 1944 at a cost of more than $102,000, and it was used to house post-polio patients, as well as central supply and an assembly room for the medical staff.

Shortly after World War II the hospital closed its obstetrics ward and east wing after notification from the State Department of Hospitals that the structures were not earthquake-safe. This reduced the hospital's bed capacity by 30 to 40 beds and helped foster plans for new medical facilities.

CLOSER COMMUNITY TIES

(1948-1969) Responding to the need for a closer relationship with the community it served, the hospital association converted from a private stock corporation to a nonprofit community hospital in early 1948, known as San Pedro Community Hospital. The new entity was directed by a board of trustees—12 laymen and three physicians—all serving without pay.

During the 1950s plans progressed for new facilities to be built at 1300 West Seventh Street. Fund-raising through public subscription began in 1957, with a $2.8 million goal. Ground breaking for the five-story structure was on June 7, 1959, and the building was dedicated less than two years later, on March 19, 1961.

San Pedro Community Hospital now had 140 beds, 65 active physicians on

Mary Jane Currie, R.N., first administrator of San Pedro General Hospital.

staff, 4 surgery rooms, and a cobalt room for radiation therapy. In the late 1960s several new departments were established: radiation therapy in 1965, a coronary care unit in 1966, and a telemetry unit in 1968.

Steady growth in the region once again helped the hospital outgrow its relatively new plant. A new master plan then called for the eventual development of a 400-bed hospital to serve San Pedro and the peninsula communities.

EAST, WEST WINGS TAKE SHAPE

(1970-present) The 1970s gave the hospital an entirely different look. Ground breaking for the new west wing was held in March 1970, and the project was completed by November 1971, boosting bed capacity of the facility to 243. At the same time a three-year-long, floor-by-floor remodeling was done, and hospital parking was expanded. The new 50,000-square-foot east wing was built from 1977 to 1979. Total cost of the expansion project was $6.6 million.

After construction the hospital—renamed San Pedro and Peninsula Hospital—housed 22 departments. These included new coronary and intensive care units, surgical suites, a new obstetrical department, an expanded radiology department, physical and inhalation therapy, and streamlined support services.

Today San Pedro Peninsula Hospital (the "and" was dropped) offers the

Today San Pedro Peninsula Hospital offers community members a full range of inpatient, outpatient, and surgical services.

Ground-breaking ceremonies for a new five-story, 50,000-square-foot east wing addition were held on March 11, 1977. The new wing was one of numerous expansion projects completed at the hospital.

professional expertise of more than 130 local physicians, 750 full-time employees, and 210 volunteers. With 436 beds, it is one of the 25 largest hospitals in the Los Angeles area.

Among its centers of excellence are emergency care, ambulatory care, chemical dependency treatment, maternal and child health, cardiovascular, industrial care, breast imaging, and rehabilitation care—a full continuum of medical services.

In addition to its wide range of in-patient, outpatient, and surgical services, San Pedro Peninsula Hospital also offers the skilled nursing services of its Pavilion, an out-of-hospital facility for recovering patients, and San Pedro Peninsula Home Care and Hospice, which makes more than 2,000 patient visits each month to provide care at home.

During six decades of change San Pedro Peninsula Hospital has been quick to respond to the health care needs of the communities it serves.

California Cotton Fumigating Co., Inc.

Founded 1939
E.A. Hackett and Maurice Buckhands, Founders
Linda R. Jacobson, President
Thomas A. Jacobson, Vice-President

THREE GENERATIONS OF OWNERSHIP

OPPORTUNITY KNOCKS

(1939) The promise of pre-World War II California and the energy of Texan E.A. Hackett made for a winning combination in 1939. Young Hackett seized a business opportunity and, with his early partner, Maurice Buckhands, built it into three generations of family ownership and operation.

Hackett came to California in the early 1920s and went to work for the California Cotton Mills fumigation division in Los Angeles. When the company was divided into Northern and Southern California plants, he and Buckhands moved quickly to buy the local business, then 10 years old, renamed the firm California Cotton Fumigating Company, and established Wilmington as its home base. What they began is now one of the oldest businesses in the San Pedro Bay area and one of the most important.

FAMILY PRIDE

(1940-1972) The two men remained partners until Buckhands' death in 1953, when Hackett bought his partner's interest from his widow. In turn, when Hackett died in 1972, he left the firm to his daughter, Linda, and her husband, Tom Jacobson. Both have been actively involved in operations since the late 1950s. "I grew up in the business," Linda notes. "As an only child, I had early on-the-job training."

Linda has always found the company interesting, with lots of challenges and varied—and sometimes strange—cargoes to be handled. She recalls one childhood image: "I walked into one of our buildings and saw Quaker Puffed Wheat and Rice packed in from floor to ceiling."

That proves the point that much more than cotton passes through the firm's process. Once it "baby-sat" a horse for two weeks. Another time a 20-foot-long Fijian fertility god made the company warehouse its temporary home. And over the years a great deal of household goods for overseas military personnel has moved through Berth 155-A, the firm's home since 1965.

It is not uncommon for California Cotton to service both outbound and incoming cargo. For instance, after cotton bales are shipped out, cotton wastes and burlap bags are often sent back to be turned into felt, car mats, and carpet matting.

Containerization made California Cotton's process easier, with its compact boxes of goods. When the boxes are made of wood, however, they too are a target for fumigation prior to shipping, because officials in some ports of entry fear the introduction of wood-boring insects in the containers themselves.

This photo was taken in 1965, the year California Cotton Fumigating Company moved to Berth 155-A, still the firm's headquarters.

HANDLING MORE IMPORTS

(1972-1978) Fruit imports have increased tremendously in the past two decades, virtually all of which must be inspected as a condition of entry, and often require fumigation. It is not uncommon for the company to treat 2.5 million lugs of grapes, peaches, apricots, and plums from Chile or large amounts of holiday staples, such as chestnuts from China, each year.

Cotton surged back into prominence following a number of dormant years; in 1978 the company treated 120,000 bales for Egypt alone. This job is customized because Egypt, known worldwide for its cotton importation, requires fumigation even before the bales are loaded on ships bound for the Middle East. California Cotton's fumigating plant now handles about 200,000 bales annually for Egypt.

Other international consignees are equally cautious. A Japanese food company insists that all pancake mix be treated, German and Far Eastern purchasers of animal hides have strict requirements, and Australian buyers of sunflower seeds want all shipments fumigated to stop germination. A significant amount of cargo bound for Australia is treated daily.

California Cotton has the largest vacuum fumigation chambers on the West Coast. The company also has smaller units to handle special assignments, such as a stuffed lion sent to Los Angeles from Africa.

The company's process is mobile, too, and can be moved to specific pier areas to do a fumigation job. Its fleet of specially equipped trucks is capable

The first location of California Cotton Fumigating Co., Inc., one of the oldest businesses in the San Pedro Bay area. Photo circa 1939

of handling a complete assignment on site.

One of California Cotton's greatest challenges is fumigating a whole ship. Banana and grain ships are usually the types of vessels requiring such treatment. "The largest ship in our record books was a Japanese grain carrier of more than 63,000 tons," Linda Jacobson notes. "It took us three days and at the time was the largest fumigation job of its kind on the West Coast."

MEETING MODERN DEMANDS

(1978-present) To meet increasingly stringent health and agricultural regulations imposed by federal, state, and county agencies, California Cotton provides continuing education programs for its employees. Operating under strict U.S. Department of Agriculture regulations and supervision, and licensed by the Air Quality Control Management Board, the firm meets health and environmental needs of the 1980s and 1990s.

Keeping up with new techniques is also a challenge, according to Linda Jacobson. The company treats both delicate and perishable items success-

fully. Even fresh flowers can be tucked into fumigation chambers now to keep unwanted pests out. Roses, orchids, tulips, and exotic plants are all candidates for California Cotton's processes.

Even with new methods, it is hard work. In cotton and fruit seasons, it is a seven-day-per-week, 18-hour-per-day operation for the Jacobsons; their son, Tom Jr.; daughter-in-law, Kristine; and core of 10 regular employees. A small staff that handles huge volumes of work is a California Cotton Fumigating Co., Inc., tradition.

Green Hills Memorial Park

Established 1948
Arlene V. Gleich, President/Chief Executive Officer
Paul D. Brown, Vice President/Grounds
Donald Ray Frew, Treasurer/Director
John J. Resich, Jr., Secretary/Director
Steven A. Espolt, Assistant Secretary
Dennis Lane, Director
Robert H. Levonian, L.C.B. & Associates/Consulting
*   Engineer*

BEGINNING WITH NO END

COMMUNITY IN NEED
(1947-1948) Late in 1947 a group of San Pedro business and professional people met in a small office to discuss their community's need for a memorial interment property. There were no parks available in San Pedro. Harbor View Cemetery, an old five-acre park, had long been closed; Wilmington Cemetery was completely neglected and cast in the typical nineteenth-century style with upright marble headstones.

Through the efforts of that group, Green Hills Memorial Park was dedicated in July 1948, and the park's first interments were held. Those plots are located high on the park's rolling hills, marked by a monument.

Six employees helped the park get started its first year, including the original president, J. Burritt Smith, who was also the first engineer, formerly with Forest Lawn. Smith helped set the tone early—not for a cemetery but for a memorial park.

ESTABLISHING TRADITIONS
(1949-1956) The founders' planning, which immediately met the needs of the community, resulted in acceptance by hundreds of local families who began to make the park a family tradition. Development moved quickly with lawns, trees, gardens, shrubs, roads, and curbs defining the landscape.

The park's 120 acres include gently sloping land with quiet valleys and sweeping views that take in the east slope of the Palos Verdes Peninsula. The park's entrance is on Western Avenue in Rancho Palos Verdes, near Palos Verdes Drive North. Adjacent to the park, 25 miles of scenic drive wanders along the peninsula through wooded land with views of the cliffs and ocean.

By 1951 the first permanent building was built in the park at a cost of $25,000. Others followed in the next few years.

PARK'S NEW STATUS
(1957-1988) In 1957 the original founding organization was transferred to a California nonprofit corporation. About the same time new direction through new management spawned further development of the park.

In 1960 Arlene V. Gleich joined the company as comptroller; she became president in 1984, with a mission to help families to be as comfortable as possible in their bereavement. She believes the beauty of the park goes a long way toward meeting that goal.

Throughout its four-plus decades Green Hills has fulfilled the community's need for a quality memorial park in the South Bay, depending greatly on the dedication of its employees. Many of them have 20, 30, or 40 years of service. They work in a family atmosphere, which transcends their tasks of planning, construction, and

The undeveloped site was once the domain of desert cactus, rabbits, and coyotes.

New landscaping with handsome lawns, shrubs, and roadways grace Green Hills Memorial Park's rolling hills.

Vietnam, or Korea.

The program features outstanding aerial tributes, including F-4 Phantom Jets that perform the missing-man formation, a helicopter that drops a commemorative wreath over the ocean, and a World War II aircraft flyover. A military band with color guards from all five branches of the military makes Green Hills' program memorable.

AN OUTDOOR CATHEDRAL
(future) Currently, some 70 acres have been developed, with 6,889 mausoleum crypts, 7,775 lawn crypts, as well as urn gardens and columbariums. In the 40-plus years since Green Hills opened, 150,000 families have established their memorial estates there, and the park has held more than 51,000 services.

Looking ahead, the park's development will continue up to 150 years, building on its cultivated creative outlook. The Memorial Park's planners refer to "The Builder's Code" by Dr. Hubert Eaton, for guidance and direction: "I will build an Outdoor Cathedral, a place of sweeping lawns, of magnificent trees, of fountains and gardens that speak of the love and reverence we hold for those who have left us, a place that will offer inspiration and solace to those who visit the memorial interment site."

With its natural setting, imaginative improvements, and personal integrity, Green Hills Memorial Park continues to serve its community.

maintenance, and extends to the people they serve. The staff is committed to meeting the ethnic and socioeconomic requirements of all families who come to it.

SPECIAL PROGRAMS ABOUND
(1989-present) Each year Green Hills gives back to the community both time and dollars in support of various projects. In addition to generous donations to local schools, churches, and community-service organizations, Green Hills provides three notable memorial services.

The park is the site of an Easter sunrise service each year, offering its inspiring setting as a backdrop. Its staff works in conjunction with the Harbor Area Ecumenical Council to provide a spectacular setting and peaceful place of worship.

Veterans Day provides another opportunity to work with the community and allows veterans to pay special tribute to the military. On this and all national holidays, Green Hills traditionally raises more than 500 American flags, donated by veterans and their families.

Its annual Memorial Day celebration is one of the largest and finest in the nation. Attendance has steadily increased from year to year, reaching more than 2,000 people in 1989. The observance overlooks the Long Beach Naval Station, departure point for many troops that went to the South Pacific,

New development on Inspiration Slope provides families with their own private memorial gardens.

Hugo Neu-Proler Co.

Founded 1962

Co-venture of Hugo Neu & Sons, Inc., and Proler
*   International Corp., John E. Prudent, General Manager*

CONSERVING THE FUTURE BY RECYCLING THE PAST

NEW SCRAP-METAL PROCESS

(1962) Two specialty businesses combined forces more than 25 years ago to turn scrap metal into a viable commodity for both import and export. Hugo Neu & Sons, Inc., an established steel-scrap exporting firm based in New York, had its origins in just the opposite activity—importing scrap from Japan to the United States. When the world's steel markets reversed, and Japan and other countries called for scrap metal, the late Hugo Neu was there to fulfill those needs from the United States as an exporter.

About the time Neu identified the market shift, Herman Proler and his brothers, whose company, Proler International, is based in Houston, had devised remarkable technology to process scrap metal. His invention fit hand in glove with Neu's approach, and the two industrial firms combined forces to create their Los Angeles business. They named their joint venture Hugo

Neu-Proler Co., and it served the area's two major ports, Los Angeles and Long Beach.

Proler International had responded

The West Coast's largest hydraulic shear—rated at 2,000 pounds—which cuts up to two-inch-thick pieces of steel into smaller, more transportable pieces.

to a U.S. government request during the Korean War to supply shredded tin cans for the American copper industry. Proler enlarged this tin-can shredder so that it could shred whole automobiles and convert them into homogeneously shredded fist-size pieces of steel, later patented and called Prolerized scrap. Since its installation in 1962, the Prolerizer has been recognized as the most innovative method of recycling derelict automobiles and countless other discarded household appliances, which otherwise would litter the streets and countryside.

Introduced along with the Prolerizer was a unique method for loading scrap metal into oceangoing bulk carriers. Prior to 1962 scrap had been loaded aboard ships with cranes and magnets. In 1962 Hugo Neu-Proler revolutionized ship loading by designing and constructing the first apron-mounted steel belt conveyor for bulk loading all grades of scrap metal into awaiting vessels. Once stowed under the decks of ships by hand to utilize all available space, scrap metal is currently automatically conveyed into spaces

An eight-foot-wide conveyor leading up to the largest, most powerful metal shredder of its kind: the Prolerizer.

beneath the vessels' decks.

INNOVATION CONTINUES

(1963-1985) One of Hugo Neu-Proler's strengths has been the use of innovative technology and processes throughout the years. The firm conducted a major computer-automation effort in 1985, updating the Prolerizer with solid-state computer controls.

The computer simultaneously monitors all aspects of the shredding process, from motor load to finished product flow, periodically altering each phase of the process to ensure continuity in the production line.

The introduction of computer technology, coupled with an electronically controlled feed system and a fleet of modern scrap-handling equipment, have all contributed to make the Prolerizer the most productive shredder on the West Coast. Annually it shreds more than 200,000 abandoned automobiles and 135,000 net tons of discarded household appliances and other assorted light-gauge metal.

In 1986 a 2,000-ton shear was installed to improve the firm's overall scrap-handling capability by providing a method to process heavier gauge metal-bearing items unsuitable for shredding.

HELPING THE ENVIRONMENT AND ECONOMY

Scrap metal has become a mainstay in modern recycling efforts, especially at Hugo Neu-Proler's main operations yard on Terminal Island. The private company's facility is the largest scrap-metal recycler and exporter on the West Coast, annually recycling and exporting more than one million net tons, which represent more than 60 percent of the region's discarded scrap metal.

The total scope of operations includes buying, transporting, processing, and stockpiling scrap metal, as well as ongoing research to develop and implement the technology that will guarantee the firm's commitment to meet the recycling needs of the community well into the next century.

Instead of being included in the solid-waste stream and straining the demands on the state's landfills, the one million net tons processed and exported by the company are recycled into high-grade scrap metal for use in the manufacture of new steel. The Environmental Protection Agency has identified several major benefits when scrap iron and steel are used instead of iron ore and coal in the making of new steel, among them a 90 percent saving in iron ore and coal reserves, a 74 percent saving in energy consumption, and a 96 percent reduction in air pollution.

In addition to its all-important environmental role, the firm makes significant contributions to employment opportunities and to the overall economy of the region. Hugo Neu-Proler directly employs 193 people and indirectly affects 2,000 additional people such as small neighborhood collectors and large independent dealers who collect a large amount of the scrap, truckers who haul the material, and others in associated businesses. The company's activities also generate millions of dollars in revenue to the Port of Los Angeles and to the many ancillary businesses associated with its operations. Finally, Hugo Neu-Proler's exports help to reduce the nation's trade deficit.

The technology advances in processing, handling, transporting, and shipping the metallic waste generated by Southern Californians, and the availability of the necessary waterfront location in the Port of Los Angeles for its operations, have catapulted the firm into the position of being the nation's leader in scrap-metal recycling and exporting. Hugo Neu-Proler Co. ensures that the past will be the foundation on which tomorrow is built.

This conveyor is used to move shredded metal through a cleaning process and onto the stockpile.

Evergreen Marine Corp.

Established 1968 by Yung-Fa Chang, Chairman
K.H. Chang, President

U.S. Agency
Evergreen International (USA) Corp.
Captain S.Y. Kuo, Vice Chairman/New York
William Wang, Vice Chairman/Los Angeles
Richard Huang, President

FIRST-CLASS SHIPPING SERVICES WORLDWIDE

LAUNCHING NUMBER ONE

(1968-1974) On September 20, 1968, Chang Yung-Fa realized a lifelong dream: He launched his international shipping business from his homeland of Taiwan with one chartered vessel. Chang, who was educated in business and architecture, personally got involved with his fledgling steamship company by qualifying as a vessel master and going to sea.

His venture, headquartered in Taipei, Taiwan, was so successful that after the first couple of years Chang went from chartering to owning and operating Evergreen's own containerships.

Evergreen's first route was from Taiwan to the Persian Gulf; then the network grew rapidly to service other markets.

COVERING THE GLOBE

(1975-1985) Service from Taiwan to the U.S. Atlantic Coast was launched in 1975, and to the West Coast two years later.

One of the most significant Evergreen operations took place in July 1984, when the company initiated an unprecedented two-way, around-the-world, regular weekly full-container service which has not been duplicated.

The service has ultramodern G-type, GL, and GX vessels sailing among its fleet in both directions and calls at Los Angeles.

The service provides a shipping system with several service routes linking exporters and importers in Asia, Europe, and America. Evergreen also remains a feeder network of containerships to nearby ports in each region and uses an inland transportation network to create a total intermodal system. In addition, Evergreen maintains separate transpacific services.

By May 1985, with an ever-more-prosperous Mediterranean market in place, Evergreen inaugurated a service from the Far East to the Red Sea and East Mediterranean. It opened up new marketing possibilities for clients in Asia and southern Europe.

INCREASED TRADE

(1986-1988) As trade between the Far East and the U.S. West Coast increased, Evergreen enhanced its three major lines on the transpacific route and had dedicated operations complemented by the around-the-world service. From Taiwan and Hong Kong, Evergreen provided weekly sailings.

In February 1986 Evergreen began

Evergreen vessels are a familiar sight in many harbors around the globe.

Double-stack trains provide intermodal service from the Los Angeles/San Pedro area.

altering its Korea/Japan/Pacific North-west service with sailings every seven days to shorten transit lines across the Pacific.

Total present Evergreen operations encompass six regular full container services: eastbound around the world, westbound around the world, Taiwan/Hong Kong/U.S. West Coast, Japan/Pacific Northwest, Far East/Mediterranean, and western Mediterranean/U.S. East Coast. There are also feeder services in Southeast Asia.

Introduction of the first Evergreen double-stack train service in the United States in July 1986 was a breakthrough in land transportation, adding speed and reliability. (A second and third were added in February and April 1988.) This transfers containers weekly between Los Angeles and various points in the United States, including the Midwest, the East Coast, and the Gulf.

SMOOTH AND EFFICIENT
(1989-present) Chang, fluent in a number of languages, is known as a

very private person. His three sons and his daughter's husband join him in business today. The chairman travels a great deal, meeting with government officials and port authorities in countries where Evergreen has offices.

There are currently 22 Evergreen offices nationwide, and numerous offices and agencies in other countries around the globe. Evergreen has some 3,000 seagoing and shore-based employees and a fleet of 62 ships that can handle up to 4,000 TEUs (Twenty-Foot Equivalent Units). Many of the ships fly the Taiwan, Republic of China, flag.

The U.S. agency, Evergreen International (USA) Corp., is head-quartered in an Evergreen-owned, 17-story office building in Jersey City, New Jersey. The company's business is to provide a fast, reliable, and economic transportation system for customers in international trade. Evergreen continuously improves techniques and adds routes, modernizes ships, and develops communications and data links as technologies

emerge to increase the scope of its service.

In San Pedro, Evergreen has two facilities: offices at 260 West Fifth Street and the Seaside Terminal on Terminal Island. The latter is fully automated and indicative of Evergreen's performance. It has grown from 25 acres to 118 acres in 12 years, and is a showcase for Evergreen's functional and economical approach to shipping containers.

Evergreen Marine Corp. has made its mark on the worldwide shipping scene, holding a significant part of the market share by serving a wide variety of industries. The company's past is prologue to its future, with efficiency and economy as the cornerstone of

Chang's philosophy.

In the mid-1980s Chang had streamlined and automated his vessels to run smoothly with a crew of 14 people, instead of the customary 45 or 50, even though the ships carry more cargo. Through quality maintenance at the dock, his system averts costly work to be done at sea, and his conscientious replacement of ships after 15 years of use retires vessels before they reach obsolescence.

Chang has diversified his business interests to include container maintenance and construction tracking and recently announced the development of an international airline, EVA Airways, which has ordered $3.6 billion worth of aircraft from U.S. suppliers.

The *Ever Given*, part of Evergreen's Round-the-World fleet.

Southwest Marine, Inc.

Founded 1977

Art Engel, Founder, President, and Chief Executive Officer

Herb Engel, Executive Vice President/General Manager,
  San Diego

David Engel, Sr., Senior Vice President/General Manager,
  San Pedro

Bill Johnston, Senior Vice President/General Manager,
  Portland

Carl Hanson, Senior Vice President/General Manager,
  San Francisco

LARGEST SHIP REPAIR YARD ON THE WEST COAST

Art Engel, one of the founders of Southwest Marine, serves as president and chief executive officer.

LONG ON EXPERIENCE

(1977-1981) Southwest Marine, Inc., was founded by Art Engel, former head of Triple A Ship Repair, an operation started by his father many years earlier. He was soon joined by his brothers, Herb and David, to create a $100-million ship repair company. At the time the eldest of the partners was 30 years old, but each had already gained valuable experience growing up with the business.

The Engel brothers' work with their father, Herbert Sr., in his Triple A shipyard in San Francisco served them well when they started their own venture. In 1977 they pooled their savings and, with Bill Johnston, formed Southwest Marine in Chula Vista, south of San Diego.

The company's first contract was to refurbish U.S. Navy landing craft, and the partners did much of the work themselves. They scraped barnacles from vessels and did myriad other tasks to get the job done and get the company off to a good start.

One year later Southwest moved into San Francisco at Pier 28, purchasing a yard there to work once again with the U.S. Navy as a major customer.

From 1978 to 1981 Southwest Marine grew to become a solid corporation with the reputation as a major yard in ship repair. A privately held company, it is structured with few managerial layers to make decisions quickly in a fast-moving industry.

SAN PEDRO STARTS UP

(1981-1985) In 1981 the company acquired the former Bethlehem Steel shipyard in Los Angeles Harbor, following its early game plan to expand. The San Pedro division started up with 10 employees. By 1985 it had gone from zero to $50 million in revenues and an expanded work force of hundreds of people, depending on the size of the jobs in the yard.

Division management points to teamwork applied at all levels as the reason for its meteoric success, and it notes a close-knit atmosphere in the yard that stems from San Pedro's waterfront flavor that still exists today.

Four years later Southwest Marine continued its expansion program by acquiring a facility in Pago Pago, American Samoa, in its continuing effort to service ships from around the world.

The business grew rapidly from scraping barnacles off ships to servicing super tankers of up to 265,000 dead-weight tons on 1,500 feet of berthing space at the San Pedro site.

COVERING THE WEST COAST

(1986-1989) In the last half of the 1980s, a large amount of Southwest Marine's work was for the U.S. Navy, but also for commercial foreign and domestic ships.

The company's successful expansion efforts stem from a people-oriented philosophy the partners share. Their business plan emphasized from the start the importance of maintaining harmonious labor relations with their employees, providing health and welfare benefits for workers, and holding regular meetings to discuss suggestions, changes of procedures, or other employee concerns.

In April 1989 the company covered more of the West Coast by acquiring Northwest Marine Iron Works in Portland, Oregon.

DIVERSITY IS NAME OF GAME

(present) The San Pedro shipyard, on Terminal Island off Los Angeles Harbor at the mouth of the main channel,

The complex overhaul of the combatant ship USS *Jarrett* (FF6-33) was a first for any West Coast shipyard. To accommodate a new, heavier antisubmarine helicopter, the ship was lengthened, reconfigured, and structurally strengthened. An extensive electronics modernization, a new antiroll device for crew comfort, and new submarine detection gear also were included in the work.

prides itself on diversity of projects. As a full-service facility it is capable of drydocking 95 percent of the world's ships.

A fluid, nonrepetitive business, the company fixes things according to the customer's need, using 15 specialized trades to do so, including electricians, pipe fitters, welders, painters, machinists, sheet-metal workers, carpenters, and calibration experts.

Currently the San Pedro division services the U.S. Navy's *Wabash* and *Roanoke* (ammunition and oil replenishers), and three landing ships— the *Fresno, Racine,* and *Cayuga.* The maintenance, done every 18 months, brings the ships up to material readiness.

The company's first yard, today's San Diego division, is corporate headquarters, with a shipyard on San Diego Bay. It encompasses 20 acres of property and more than 36 acres of water area. With five piers, two dry docks, and three marine railways, the modern facility performs any type of repair or refurbishing.

San Francisco's division, in the hub of the Bay Area's shipping industry, provides pier space and full services for ships of all sizes. The division's place in the world port and proximity to the metropolitan area nearby enhances its abil-

An aerial view of Southwest Marine's San Pedro facility, with a variety of ships in for repair.

ity for fast delivery of parts and accessories from around the world.

The Samoan division now has two marine railways with capacities of 800 and 3,000 tons. Ships in dock and alongside the repair berth are serviced by hydraulic land cranes with heavy tonnage capacity and are supplied with all hotel services as well. And the yard has fully equipped shops with machine, electrical, and carpentry capabilities.

A major challenge of the 1990s for

Southwest Marine, Inc., is to meet the changing environmental landscape with new techniques and new technologies. Complexities in local, state, and federal regulations have proliferated since the company's founding.

Based on a business that has grown by thirtyfold in a little over a dozen years, Southwest Marine, Inc., is making a long-term commitment to San Pedro through another 20-year lease with the port.

Los Angeles Maritime Museum

Established 1979
William B. Lee, Ph.D., Director

CELEBRATING CALIFORNIA'S SEAFARERS

The Los Angeles Maritime Museum is housed in the former Municipal Ferry Building at Berth 84, at the foot of Sixth Street in San Pedro.

IN THE HEART OF THE PORT

(1979-1983) When Los Angeles celebrated its bicentennial in 1979, the city's Maritime Museum came to life. The museum opened its doors at Berth 84 at the foot of Sixth Street in San Pedro to chronicle the rich history of the port and serve as archives for California's development through seafaring activity.

"Hollywood would like us to think everyone came overland by wagon train," says Dr. William B. Lee, the museum's director. "Not so. Most pioneers came by ship—the cheapest and fastest route until the railroad was in place."

The museum is housed in the former Municipal Ferry Building, constructed in 1941, which linked San Pedro with Terminal Island. Its doors open directly onto the main ship channel, allowing visitors a firsthand look at the constantly changing panorama.

When the ferries ran from this building, now a historical cultural monument, thousands of people went through each day—it was the only way to get to Terminal Island and major shipbuilding activity before the Vincent Thomas Bridge was built.

From the start, the museum has emphasized the history of transportation on the Pacific Ocean and the development of the port through which so much of the nation's goods enter. Even the early explorers, Juan Rodriguez Cabrillo (1542) among them, used the

The museum is staffed by professionals assisted by some 300 docents and volunteers.

Pacific as their highway and brought to California a lasting maritime heritage for future generations to enjoy.

A LIVING MUSEUM

(1983-1985) In 1983 the Los Angeles Maritime Museum became part of the Department of Parks and Recreation of the City of Los Angeles. With its own dock and a wall of windows overlooking the ship channel, the living museum plays host to visiting ships as part of its floating museum. These ships range from contemporary craft to reproductions of historic models. The Los Angeles Maritime Museum's waterfront location sets it apart from other similar institutions, which are often inland.

PROFESSIONAL STAFF ON BOARD

(1986-present) The department's decision to recruit a professional staff was a definite turning point in the museum's development. Lee became director in 1986, then hired a full-time librarian in 1987 and a curator in 1989. The staff totals nine full-time employees and is assisted by some 300 volunteers and docents.

Eighty percent of today's exhibits are models, with some 350 presenting a fascinating mix of maritime history. Relics from the USS *Los Angeles,* which was scrapped there in the 1970s, now rest at the Los Angeles Maritime Museum, including its main mast and bow peak.

Visitors number an annual 110,000 people (14,000 of them schoolchildren), taking tours or classes in nautical studies and learning to enjoy the wonderful world of ships.

A fascinating mix of maritime history is presented to 14,000 schoolchildren annually.

Anderson Medical Group

Founded 1948
Dr. William R. Anderson, Founder
Dr. Maurice DeCuir, Medical Director
Sandra Lippman, B.H.H. Network, Director of Marketing
*   and Planning*
Inger Henson, Nursing Supervisor

SERVING SEAFARERS AND INDUSTRY

FIRST CLINIC IN REGION

(1948-1950) After World War II, when San Pedro became a boomtown for trade and commerce, a visionary physician set up his clinic to serve seafarers and landlubbers alike. Dr. William R. Anderson chose 593 West Sixth Street, then on the main access to San Pedro's downtown business district and to the Terminal Island Ferry, as the location that has remained constant to this day.

Dr. Anderson's place, as it was known, was the only clinic for miles, and the doctor became well known for making ship calls at all hours. An innovator in maritime medicine, Dr. Anderson established a practice that became a model for an international network that serves shipping and industrial patients worldwide.

TREATING THE TOTAL COMMUNITY

(1950-1985) Anderson Medical Group grew along with the burgeoning community in the 1950s, serving oil refineries, shipyards, and fishing, manufacturing, and foreign trade-related businesses.

Maritime unions grew, too, and became a vital part of the clinic's business.

In 1961 Dr. Anderson, with fellow doctors David Croft and Theodore Benell, hired Inger Henson, now nursing supervisor, whose long tenure is indicative of the continuity the clinic enjoys in the community.

NEW OWNER, SAME DEDICATION

(1985-present) Dr. Anthony Rippo purchased Anderson Medical Group in 1985, expanding liaisons to interact more directly with some 35 other clinics worldwide. Four years later AMG merged with Bay Harbor Hospital and, working through the BHH Occupational Network, expanded its comprehensive health care even further to cover all facets of occupational medicine for primary, specialty, and hospital care. In addition, AMG offers ancillary programs that reduce workers' compensation claims exposure while delivering high-quality medical care.

Today all the maritime unions in the ports of Los Angeles and Long Beach patronize the Anderson Medical Group for their medical needs. Other patrons include industries of all types, Military Sealife Command, and private patients.

Dr. Anderson's legacy continues with a clinic on the cutting edge of occupational medicine. Early dedication to quality care and cost efficiency specifically for the maritime and port-related industries has underscored AMG's role as model for care and treatment of both mobile and fixed employee populations worldwide.

Key to Anderson Medical Group's service are continuity of care, centralized communications, and a multilingual staff that responds with immediate care arrangements anywhere, anytime.

Anderson Medical Group has been located at 593 West Sixth Street since its founding in 1948.

Terry J. Coniglio, Inc.
A Professional Corporation

Founded 1980
Terry J. Coniglio, Principal Attorney

ADMIRALTY & MARITIME ATTORNEYS

The law firm of Terry J. Coniglio, Inc., a P.C., handles admiralty/maritime as well as general business law and litigation, both at home and abroad, especially in the Pacific Rim.

DOCKSIDE TRAINING
(1973-1978) A longtime interest in international business led Terry J. Coniglio straight from college to the docks in Houston's ship channel for his first maritime experience. He had just earned a bachelor's degree in business administration from California State University at Long Beach.

His first job was in the shipping industry with Sea-Land Service, Inc., of Menlo Park, New Jersey, and he went into its six-month training program with great enthusiasm.

"It proved invaluable," Coniglio recalls. "It gave me a concentrated overview and insights that take years to gain." The program covered marine and container operations, labor relations, regulations of the U.S. Customs Service and the Federal Maritime Commission, warehousing, distribution, and tariffs. It gave him a chance to work with longshoremen and managers alike.

In 1975 Coniglio joined Seatrain Lines, Inc., based in Weehawken, New Jersey, to become western area manager of Oakland/Long Beach operations. There he coordinated operations and sales activities for the company's Far East division, dealing with exporters, importers, freight forwarders, and customshouse brokers.

LEGAL INTEREST SURFACES
(1979-present) Although Coniglio won a number of sales awards, he wanted to go into maritime law. He took law-school classes while still employed with Seatrain and received his juris doctor degree from Western State University of Law in 1979—in the top 10 percent of his class. In 1980 he passed the bar and opened his practice in Los Angeles, working with shipping-industry clients right from the start.

Coniglio is at ease in totally different international endeavors, whether negotiating a case in a business office overlooking Sydney Harbor or litigating a matter in a local court. His extensive experience both in shipping and the law gives focus to his firm's boutique approach, handling admiralty/maritime as well as general business law and litigation. The firm's employees deal with cases at home and abroad, especially in the Pacific Rim, from offices in Long Beach and serve as both attorneys and consultants.

The practice areas of Terry J. Coniglio, Inc., involve domestic and international transportation, U.S. customs, freight, and ocean-shipping law. Typical cases include vessel seizures/attachment writs, appearances before the Federal Maritime Commission and U.S. Customs Service, dock-damage cases, cargo defense, labor law, stevedoring claims and regulation, and litigation disputes representing shipping companies against general agents, shippers, or consignees. And the list goes on.

Coniglio's professional memberships include the U.S. Court of International Trade, State Bar of California, and the Maritime Law Association of the United States, in which he is a proctor in admiralty.

Terry J. Coniglio

Patrons

The following individuals, companies, and organizations have made a valuable commitment to the quality of this publication. Windsor Publications and the Los Angeles Maritime Museum gratefully acknowledge their participation in *The San Pedro Bay Area: Headlines in History.*

Anderson Medical Group*
California Cotton Fumigating Co., Inc.*
Terry J. Coniglio, Inc.*
Evergreen Marine Corp.*
Fellows & Stewart Company*
Green Hills Memorial Park*
Hugo Neu-Proler Co.*
Al Larson Boat Shop*
Metropolitan Stevedore Company*
Port of Long Beach*
San Pedro Peninsula Hospital*
Southwest Marine, Inc.*
Stevedoring Services of America*
WORLDPORT LA*

*Chronicles of Enterprise of *The San Pedro Bay Area: Headlines in History.* The histories of these companies and organizations appear in Chapter 7, beginning on page 95.

Bibliography

BOOKS

Bauer, K. Jack. *The Mexican War, 1846-1848.* New York: Macmillan Publishing Company. Inc., 1974.

Berner, Loretta, ed. *The Pike on the Silverstrand.* Long Beach: Historical Society of Long Beach, 1982.

Cahn, William. *A Pictorial History of American Labor.* New York: Crown Publishers, Inc., 1972.

Case, Walter H. *History of Long Beach and Vicinity.* Chicago: The S.J. Clarke Publishing Company, 1927.

Clark, David L. *Los Angeles: A City Apart.* Woodland Hills, California: Windsor Publications, Inc., 1981.

DeAntley, Richard. *Long Beach: The Golden Shore.* Houston: Pioneer Publications, Inc., 1988.

Dubofsky, Melvyn. *We Shall Be All: A History of Syndicalism in the United States.* Chicago: Quadrangle Books, 1969.

Dulles, Foster Rhea, and Dubofsky, Melvyn. *Labor in America: A History.* 4th edition. Arlington Heights, Illinois: Harlan Davidson, Inc., 1984.

Gleason, Duncan. *The Islands and Ports of California: A Guide to Coastal California.* New York: The Devin-Adair Company, 1958.

Grenier, Judson A. *A Guide to Historic Places in Los Angeles County.* Dubuque, Iowa: Kendall/Hunt Publishing Company, 1978.

Hinckle, Warren. *The Big Strike.* Virginia City, Nevada: Silver Dollar Books, 1985.

Lens, Sidney. *The Labor Wars.* Garden City, New York: Doubleday and Co., Inc., 1973.

Meyer, Larry L., and Kalayjian, Patricia L. *Long Beach: Fortune's Harbor.* Tulsa, Oklahoma: Continental Heritage Press, 1983.

Queenan, Charles F. *Long Beach and Los Angeles: A Tale of Two Ports.* Northridge, California: Windsor Publications, Inc., 1986.

Queenan, Charles F. *The Port of Los Angeles: From Wilderness to World Port.* Los Angeles, California: Los Angeles Harbor Dept. 1983.

Silka, Henry P. *San Pedro: A Pictorial History.* San Pedro, California: San Pedro Bay Historical Society, 1984.

Vickery, Oliver. *Harbor Heritage.* Mountain View, California: Authors Book Company, 1979.

Weinman, Lois J., and Stickel, E. Gary. *Los Angeles-Long Beach Harbor Areas Cultural Resources Survey.* Los Angeles: U.S. Army Corps of Engineers, Los Angeles District, 1978.

PERIODICALS

Almeida, Art. "How San Pedro Killed the Wobblies." *California Magazine,* July/August 1984.

Felice, Marc. "25 Years of Containerization." *Transport 2000,* May/June 1981.

Holstrom, David. "Long Beach is Sinking." *The Elks Magazine,* May 1989.

Ingram, Susan. "Women Man Homefront." *Long Beach Heritage,* 3:2 (May 1982).

International Longshoremen's and Warehousemen's Union. *The Dispatcher,* 42:7 (July 6, 1984).

McKinney, Elizabeth. "San Pedro Golf and Country Club—A Paradise Lost." *The Shoreline. San Pedro Bay Historical Society,* September 1982.

Port of Los Angeles. "Seafood Center." *Angels Gate Magazine,* June 1977.

"San Pedro Bathhouse." *The Shoreline. San Pedro Bay Historical Society,* June 1989.

Travis, Helen. "Bloody Thursday." *Random Lengths,* August/September 1983.

Winn, Leslie. "Douglas and Long Beach: Co-pilots in War Effort. " *Long Beach Heritage," 3:2 (May 1982).*

OTHER PUBLICATIONS

Beck, Robert F., Lemm, Timothy T., Radmilovich, Sandra, eds. *San Pedro . . . The First 100 Years.* San Pedro: Copley Los Angeles Newspapers, 1988.

Bridge Department, California Department of Highways. *The Vincent Thomas Bridge.* Sacramento: n.p., 1963.

Drum Barracks Civil War Museum. "The Great Camel Experiment." *Drumbeats,* III:4, (October 1988).

Long Beach Independent/Press-Telegram. *Parade of Progress,* January 2, 1958.

Long Beach Naval Shipyard Employees Association, Inc. *The Case for the Long Beach Naval Shipyard.* Long Beach: n.p., 1955.

Schwartz, Michael, Wigginton, Vicki, Kirkendall, Mike, eds. *Long Beach Centennial: History by the Sea.* Long Beach: Long Beach Press Telegram, March 20, 1988.

Wentz, John Budd. *An Analysis of the Advisability of Annexing All or a Part of the Lakewood Area to the City of Long Beach.* Long Beach: City of Long Beach, July 1951.

Yamashita, Dr. Kanshi Stanley. "East San Pedro, Story of an Ethnic Fishing Community." *San Pedro Traditions Festival,* San Pedro: City of Los Angeles Cultural Affairs Department, February 12, 1989.

LIBRARIES AND ARCHIVES

City of Long Beach Public Library, Main Branch, Research Section, Historical Files

City of Los Angeles Public Library, San Pedro Branch, Historical Section Files

Port of Long Beach, Communications Division, Historical Files Section

Photo Credits

Index

About the Contributors

THE AUTHOR
Stephen T. Sato is a Communications Specialist for the Port of Long Beach and a longtime resident of the South Bay area. A member of the San Pedro Bay Master Plan Steering Committee and author of a series of business histories that appeared in Windsor Publication's *Long Beach and Los Angeles: A Tale of Two Ports,* Sato is uniquely qualified to write a history of the San Pedro Bay area. This former newspaper writer, newsletter editor, and U.S. Army public information officer has long been interested in the history of the San Pedro Bay area.

THE "CHRONICLES OF ENTERPRISE" WRITER
Cynthia Simone is a Southern California-based business writer specializing in corporate and marketing communications. As an editor, writer, and photographer, her professional experience includes working with a variety of industries. Through Simone Communications, which she established in 1982, she provides creative editorial services for clients, many of whom have international interests.

THE PHOTO RESEARCHER
Charles F. Queenan is a longtime journalist, publicist, photo researcher, and published author of the Los Angeles Harbor Department's *The Port of Los Angeles: From Wilderness to World Port* and Windsor's *Long Beach and Los Angeles: A Tale of Two Ports.* In addition, Queenan has written corporate histories of the U.S. operations of Toyota and Datsun and a history of Caesar's World.